The Science Quest

Physics, Biology, and Chemistry for Class 10th

Complete Guide to Mastering Science

Written by Faizan Ahmad Bhat

Edited and Prepared by JD

Self-Published:2025

Copyright Page

Dedication

To my students, Your curiosity and enthusiasm for science light the way.

Foreword

By Faizan Bhat ,Teacher and Author As a teacher, I've seen how science can spark wonder in young minds. The Science Quest is my effort to make Physics, Biology, and Chemistry accessible and exciting for Class 10 students. This book blends clear explanations with practical examples, guiding learners through the complexities of science with ease. With JD's invaluable help in editing and shaping it, I hope it becomes not just a textbook, but a doorway to discovery. I'm confident it will inspire students to explore, question, and excel. Happy learning!

Preface

Welcome to The Science Quest! I wrote this book to bring Physics, Biology, and Chemistry together in one place, making it easier and more exciting for 10th-grade students like you to explore the wonders of science. Whether it's understanding how a rocket moves, how plants breathe, or how chemicals react, this book is your guide to mastering these subjects. Thanks to JD for editing and preparing it—with clear explanations, diagrams, and practice questions, I hope you'll find science not just a subject to study, but a world to discover. Let's dive in!—Faizan Ahmad

Editor's Note

By JD Bringing The Science Quest to life has been a rewarding journey. As the editor and preparer, I've worked to shape Faizan Ahmad's brilliant content into a book that's clear, engaging, and easy to use for Class 10 students. From typing it up in MS Word to organizing the layout, my goal was to ensure every diagram, example, and question supports your learning. Science is a team effort, and I'm proud to play my part in helping you unlock its wonders. Enjoy the ride!—JD

If you are also a Author I will shape your work into a book contact us

@ IG | (junnaid0)

Email [junaidulislam484@gmail,com]

Contents

Physics

Light
Human Eye
Electricity
Magnetic Effects of Electric Current

Chemistry

Chemical Reactions and Equations
Carbon and its Compounds
Metals and Non-Metals
Acids, Bases, and Salts

Biology

Life Processes -
Control and Coordination
Reproduction
Heredity
Our Environment

Introduction

Science is everywhere—from the phone in your hand to the air you breathe. This book, The Science Quest, combines Physics, Biology, and Chemistry into one adventure for Class 10 students. Each section follows your syllabus and is packed with examples, diagrams, and questions to help you learn and succeed. Physics will show you how the world moves, Biology will uncover the secrets of life, and Chemistry will reveal how matter transforms. Read actively, try the exercises, and ask questions—science is yours to unlock!

How to Use This Book

- Chapters: Each one covers a key topic with explanations, diagrams, and solved examples.

- Practice: Test yourself with questions at the end of each chapter.

- Extras: Use the glossary for quick definitions and the index to find topics fast.

- Tip: Take notes and revisit tough sections—practice makes perfct

Light – Reflection & Refraction

Rectilinear propagation of light - light travels in a straight line· Speed of Light = c = 3×10^8 m/s

Reflection: The bouncing back of light from any shiny surface in the same medium e.g. mirror or water. The study of light is called OPTICS

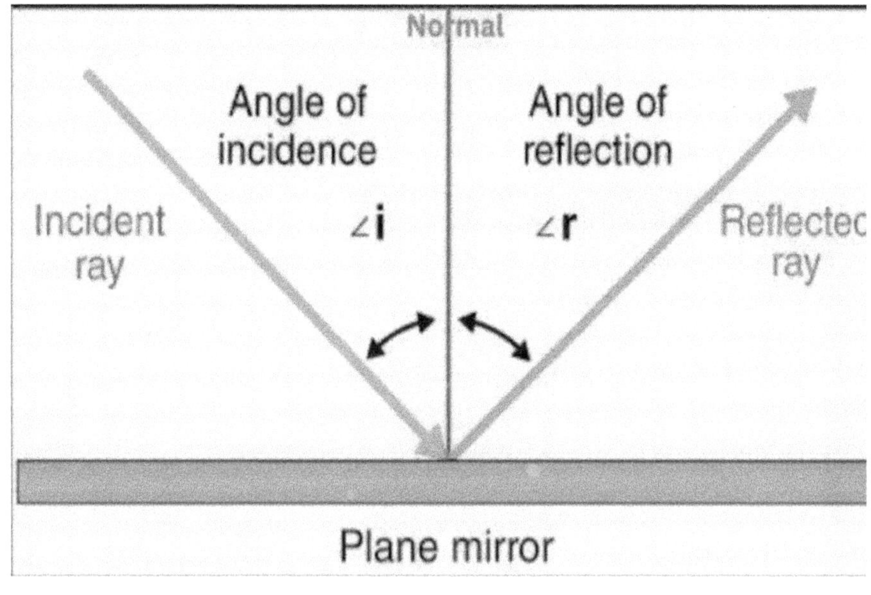

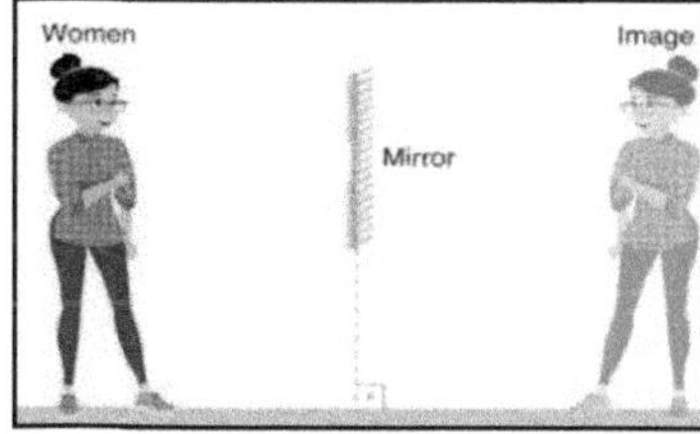

The Laws of reflection states that:

1.   The Incident ray, the Reflected ray and Normal all lie in the same plane.

2.   Angle of incidence (∠i) = Angle of reflection (∠r).

Plane mirror: The mirror whose reflecting surface is plane.

The image formed by a plane mirror is =

- Always virtual and erect.
- Size of the image is equal to that of the object
- image formed is as far behind the mirror as the object is in front of it
- image is Laterally inverted (lateral inversion)

Spherical Mirror: Mirror whose reflecting surface is Curved .

CONCAVE MIRROR = reflecting surface is curved inwards, towards the center of the sphere

CONVEX MIRROR =reflecting surface is curved outwards.

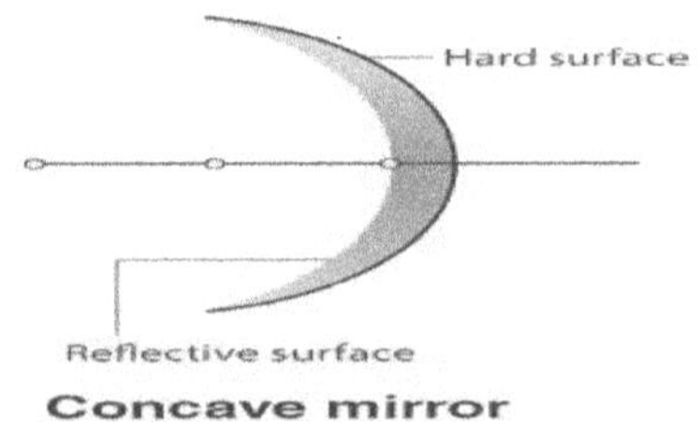

Terms	Definition	
Pole (P)	The center point of the reflecting surface of a spherical mirror	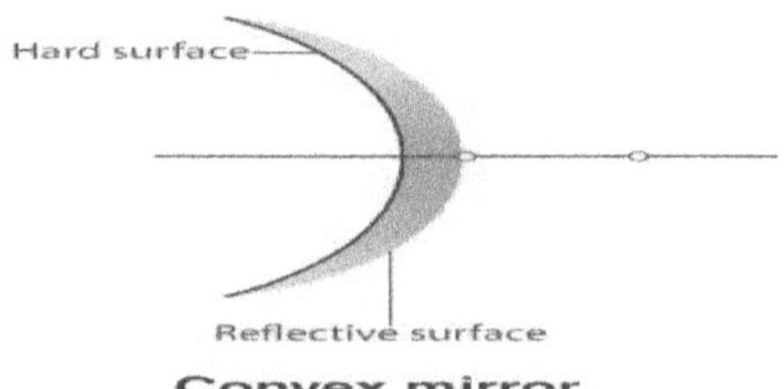
Centre of Curvature (C)	The center of the sphere of which the mirror's reflecting surface forms a part	
Radius of Curvature (R)	The radius of the sphere of which the mirror's reflecting surface forms a part	CONCAVE MIRROR R = 2f
Principal Axis	The straight line passing through the pole and the center of curvature of the mirror	
Principal Focus (F)	The point where parallel rays of light either converge or appear to diverge after reflecting from the mirror	

| **Focal Length (f)** | The distance between the pole and the principal focus |
| **Aperture** | The diameter of the reflecting surface of the spherical mirror |

Ray Diagrams

(i) A ray parallel to principal axis will pass through focus after reflection.

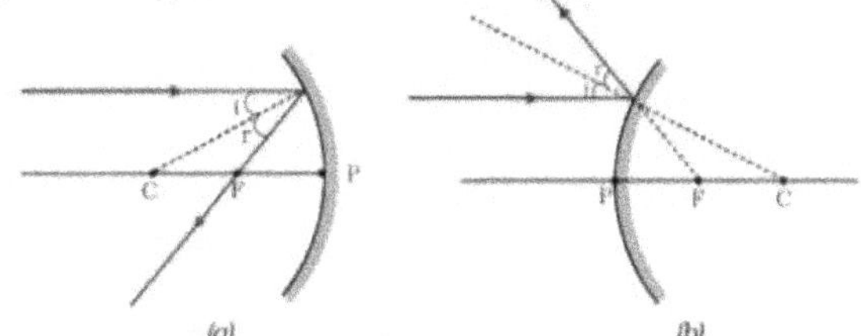

(ii) A ray passing through the principal focus will become parallel to principal axis after reflection

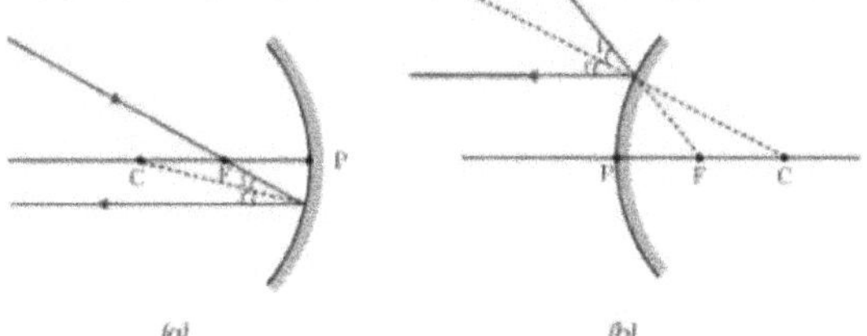

(iii) A ray passing through center of curvature will follow the same path back after reflection.

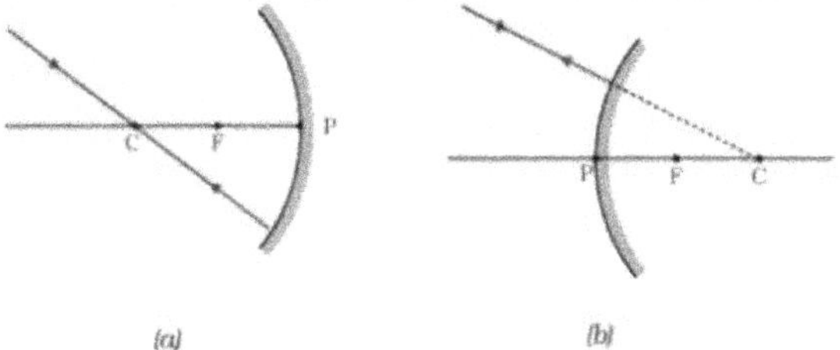

(iv) Ray incident at pole is reflected back making same angle with principal axis.

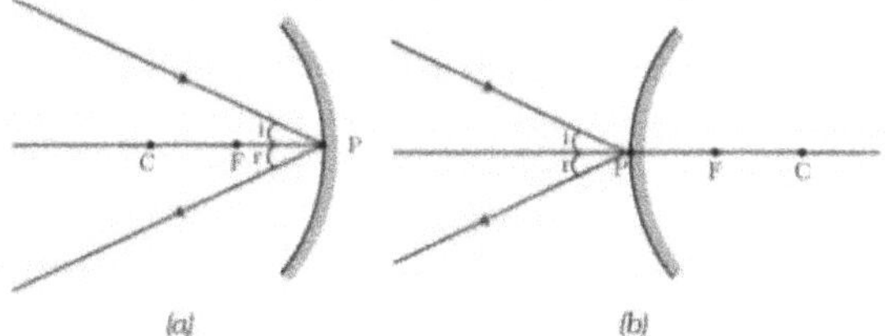

Concave Mirror

Position of the object	Position of the image	Size of the image	Nature of the image
At infinity	At the focus F	Highly diminished point-sized	Real and inverted
Beyond C	Between F and C	Diminished	Real and inverted

At C	At C	Same size	Real and inverted
Between C and F	Beyond C	Enlarged	Real and inverted
At F	At infinity	Highly enlarged	Real and inverted
Between P and F	Behind the mirror	Enlarged	Virtual and erect

Uses of Concave Mirrors:

- Torches

- Shaving Mirrors

- Dentist's Mirror

Convex Mirror

Position of the object	Position of the image	Size of the image	Nature of the image
At infinity	At the focus F behind the mirror	Highly diminished point-sized	Virtual and erect
Between infinity and the pole P of the mirror	Between P and F behind the mirror	Diminished	Virtual and erect

Uses of Convex Mirrors

- Rear-view Mirrors in Vehicles

- Preferred in Vehicles:

- Provide erect, though diminished, images

- Have a wider field of view due to their outward curve

- Allow drivers to view a larger area compared   to plane mirrors

Convention	Key Terms
Object Placement	Object to the left of the mirror
Distance Measurement	Measured from the pole of the mirror
Positive x-axis	Right of origin (positive)
Negative x-axis	Left of origin (negative)
Positive y-axis	Above principal axis (positive)
Negative y-axis	Below principal axis (negative)

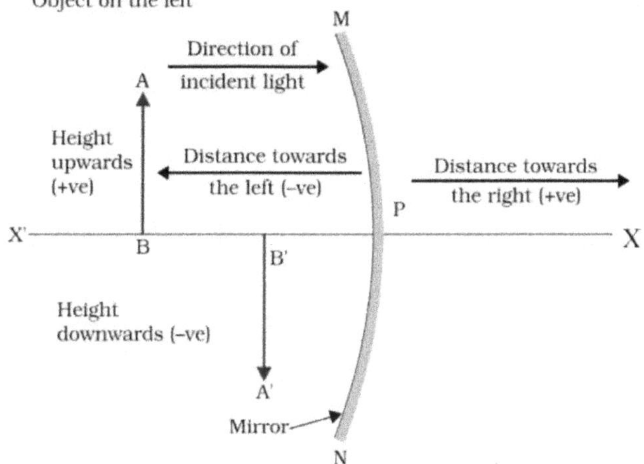

Important Formulas : Magnification refers to the ratio of the height of an image to the height of an object

Mirror Formula $1/v + 1/u = 1/f$

m = Height of image(h') / Height of object(h) = v / u

h' = positive (virtual images)

h' = negative (real images)

m = negative (real)

m = positive (virtual)

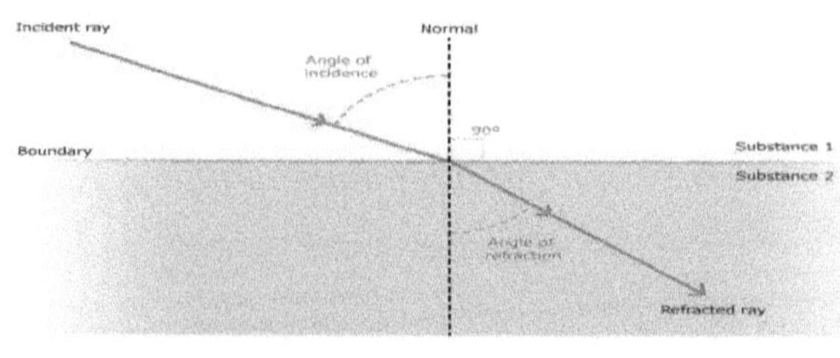

REFRACTION; the bending of light when it passes from one medium to another medium(caused due to speed difference)

Refraction of Light = Phenomenon of change in the direction of light when it passes from one transparent medium to another.

Laws of refraction of light :(i) The incident ray, the refracted ray and the normal to the interface of two transparent media at the point of incidence, all lie in the same plane.

$$\text{(ii)} \quad \frac{\sin i}{\sin r} = \text{constant}$$

Snell's law of refraction.

Refractive index : measurement of how much a light ray bends when it passes from one medium to another.

$$n_{21} = \frac{\text{Speed of light in medium 1}}{\text{Speed of light in medium 2}} = \frac{v_1}{v_2}$$

$$n_m = \frac{\text{Speed of light in air}}{\text{Speed of light in medium}} = \frac{c}{v}$$

Lenses: A transparent material bound by two surfaces, of which one or both surfaces are spherical.

Term	Meaning
Convex Lens	A lens with two spherical surfaces bulging outwards thicker in the middle than at the edges. (Converging Lens)
Concave Lens	A lens with two spherical surfaces curved inwards thicker at the edges than at the middle. (Diverging Lens)
Centre of Curvature (C C1 C2)	The center of the sphere from which the lens surface is a part.
Principal Axis	An imaginary straight line passing through the two centers of curvature of a lens.
Optical Centre (O)	The central point of a lens where a ray of light passes without deviation.

Aperture	The effective diameter of the circular outline of a spherical lens.
Principal Focus (F F2)	F1 The point where rays of light parallel to the principal axis converge (convex) or appear to diverge (concave).
Focal Length (f)	The distance between the principal focus and the optical centre of a lens.

Ray Diagram

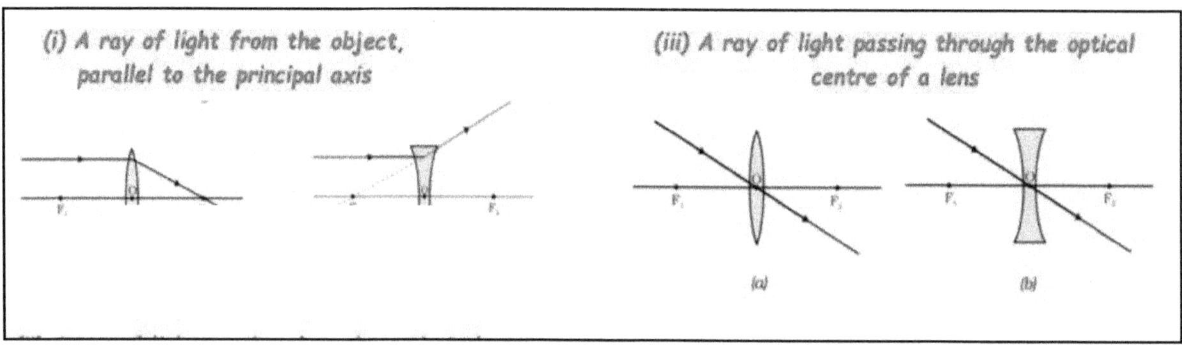

Image formation by concave and convex lense

Convex Mirror

Concave Mirror

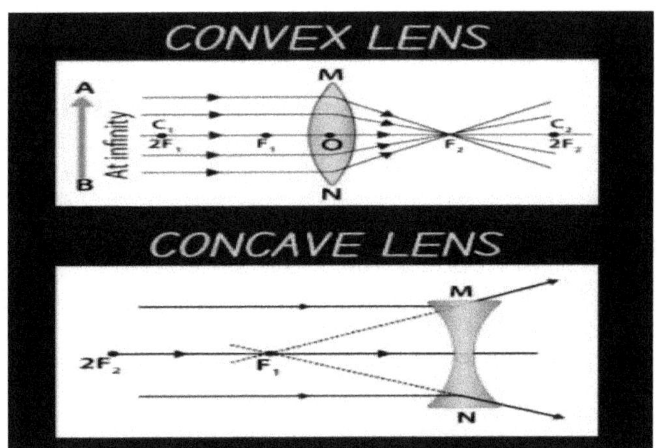

Convex Lens

Position of the object	Position of the image	Relative size of the image	Nature of the image
"At infinity"	"At focus F_2"	"Highly diminished point-sized"	"Real and inverted"
"Beyond $2F_1$"	"Between F_2 and $2F_2$"	"Diminished"	"Real and inverted"
"At $2F_1$"	"At $2F_2$"	"Same size"	"Real and inverted"
"Between F_1 and $2F_1$"	"Beyond $2F_2$"	"Enlarged"	"Real and inverted"
"At focus F_1"	"At infinity"	"Infinitely large or highly enlarged"	"Real and inverted"
"Between focus F_1 and optical centre O"	"On the same side of the lens as the object"	"Enlarged"	"Virtual and erect

Concave Lens

Position of the object	Position of the image	Relative size of the image	Nature of the image
"At infinity"	"At focus F_1"	"Highly diminished point-sized"	"Virtual and erect"
"Between infinity and optical centre	"Between focus F_1 and optical centre O"	"Diminished"	"Virtual and erect"

O"

Uses of Convex Lens:

- overhead project
- camera
- focus sunlight
- simple telescope
- projector microscope
- magnifying glasses

Uses of Concave Lens:

- spy holes in the doors
- glasses
- some telescopes

Important Formulas of Lens:

All measurements are taken from the optical centre of the lens.

focal length of a convex lens = positive, and that of a concave lens = negative.

Lens formula:

$$\frac{1}{v} - \frac{1}{u} = \frac{1}{f}$$

Magnification:

$$m = \frac{\text{Height of image}}{\text{Height of object}} = \frac{h'}{h} = \frac{v}{u}$$

Power of Lens: The ability of a lens to converge or diverge the ray of light after refraction through it is called the power of the lens. It is defined as the reciprocal of focal length.

SI unit = Dioptre (D)

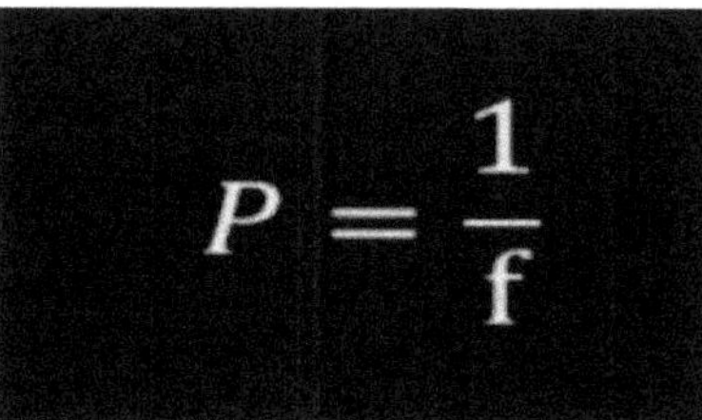

$$P = \frac{1}{f}$$

1 dioptre is the power of a lens whose focal length

is 1 metre. $1D = 1m^{-1}$

power of a convex lens = positive

power of concave lens = negative.

1. A convex mirror used for rear-view on an automobile has a radius of curvature of 3.00 m. If a bus is located at 5.00 m from this mirror, find the position, nature, and size of the image.Radius of curvature, (R = +3.00 , \text{m});Object-distance, (u = -5.00 , \text{m});Image-distance, (v = ?);Height of the image, (h' = ?);Focal length, (f = R/2 = +3.00 , \text{m} / 2 = +1.50 , \text{m}) (as the principal focus of a convex mirror is behind the mirror).

2. An object, 4.0 cm in size, is placed at 25.0 cm in front of a concave mirror of focal length 15.0 cm. At what distance from the mirror should a screen be placed in order to obtain a sharp image? Find the nature and the size of the image.Object-size, (h = +4.0 , \text{cm});Object-distance, (u = -25.0 , \text{cm});Focal length, (f = -15.0 , \text{cm});Image-distance, (v = ?);Image-size, (h' = ?).

3. A concave lens has focal length of 15 cm. At what distance should the object from the lens be placed so that it forms an image at 10 cm from the lens? Also find the magnification produced by the lens.A concave lens always forms a virtual, erect image on the same side of the object.Image-distance (v = -10 , \text{cm});Focal length (f = -15 , \text{cm});

Object-distance (u = ?).

HUMAN EYE

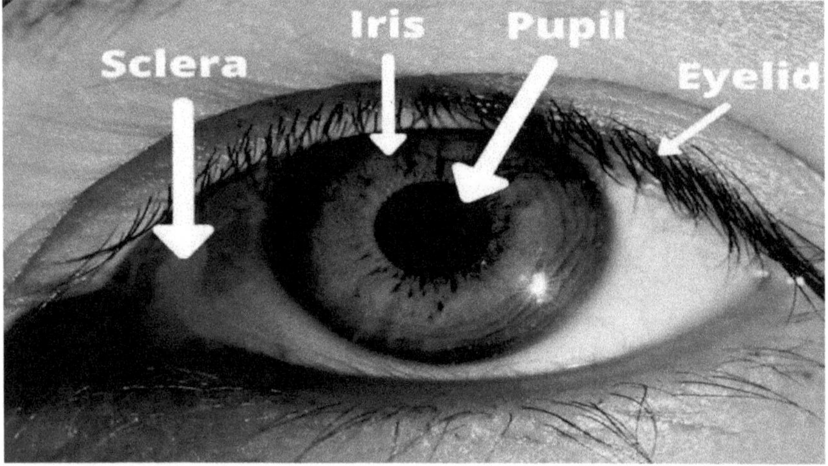

HUMAN EYE

- Sense organ that helps us to see.

- Located in eye sockets in skull.

- Diameter of Eye is 2.3 cm (Size of eye remains same throughout our whole life)

Parts of HUMAN EYE

1.**Cornea** – It is the outermost, transparent part. It provides most of the refraction of light.

2.**Lens** – It is composed of a fibrous, jelly-like material. Provides the focused real and inverted image of the object on the Retina. This is convex lens that converges light at Retina.

3.**Iris** – It is a dark muscular diaphragm that controls the size of the pupil.

4.**Pupil** – It is the window of the eye. It is the central aperture in Iris. It regulates and controls the amount of light entering the eye.

5.**Ciliary Muscles** – They hold the lens in position and help in modifying the curvature of lens.

6.**Retina** – It is a delicate membrane having enormous number of light sensitive cells.

7.**Optic Nerve** – It transmits visual information from retina to Brain.

8.**Blind Spot** – The point at which the optic nerve leaves the eye.

9.**Aqueous Humour** – Between the cornea and eye lens, there is a space filled with transparent liquid is called the aqueous humour which helps the refracted light to be focused on retina. It also provides nutrition to eye.

10.**Vitreous Humour** – Space between eye lens and retina is filled with a liquid called Vitreous Humour.

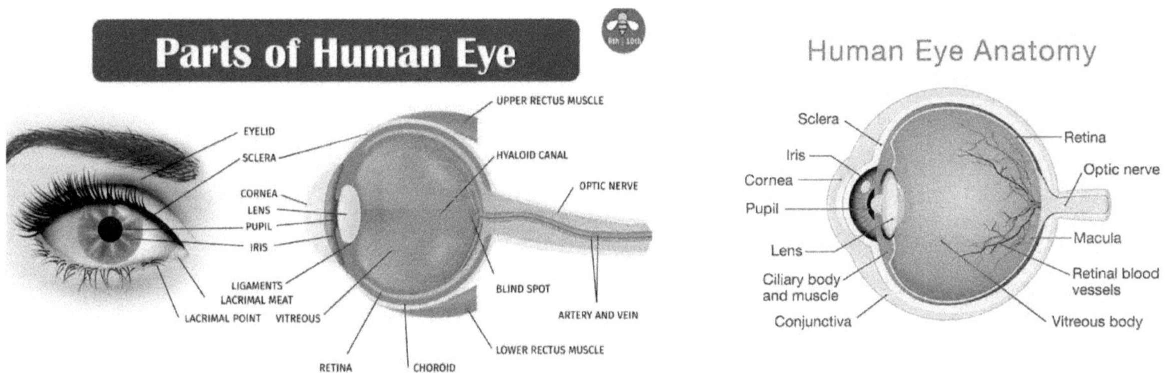

Far Point of Eye - Maximum distance to which eye can see clearly, is called far point of eye. - For a normal eye, it's value is Infinity

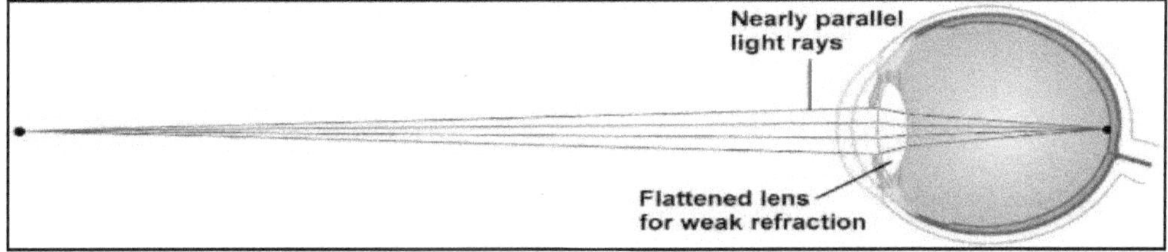

Near Point of Eye - Minimum distance at which an object can be seen most distinctly without any strain is called the least distance of distinct vision. - For a normal eye, it's value is 25cm

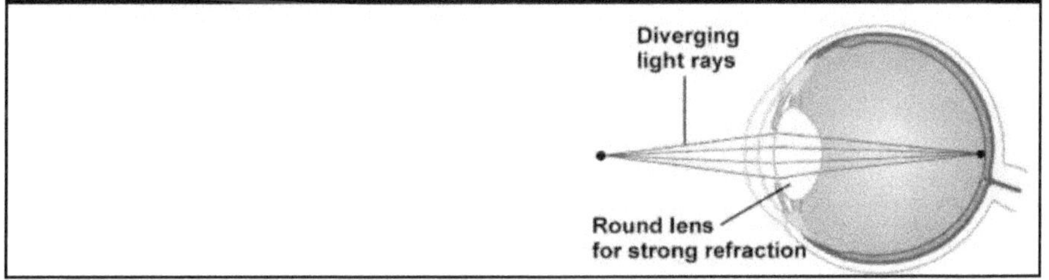

Power of Accommodation

The process by which certain muscles (called ciliary muscles) function to change the focal length of the eyes so that the image is clearly formed on the retina is called accommodation of the eye.

• If the object in consideration is at a distance, for the image to form at the retina, the focal length has to be large. Here, the ciliary muscles relax, thereby thinning the eye lens. The focal length increases and the image is formed perfectly on the retina.

• Similarly, in the case of near-lying objects, the ciliary muscles contract and thereby thickening the lens. This causes a reduction in the focal length for ideal image formation.

Range of human vision is from 25 cm to infinity

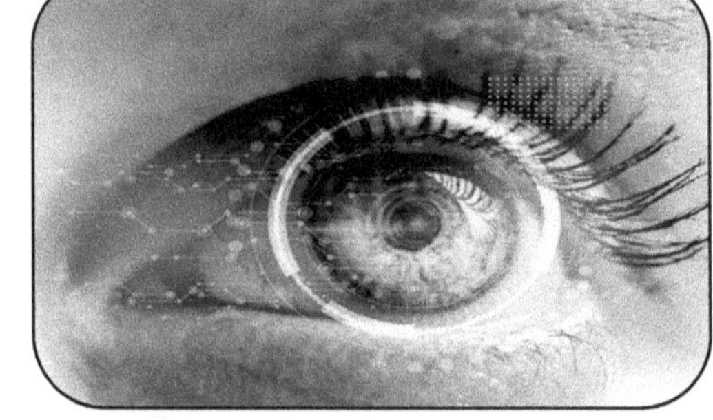

Case 1) **To see far Objects**

-      Ciliary Muscles – Relaxed

-      Eye Lens - Thin

-      Focal length - Increase

Case 2) **To see near Objects**

-      Ciliary Muscles - Contract

-      Eye Lens - Thick

-      Focal length - Decrease

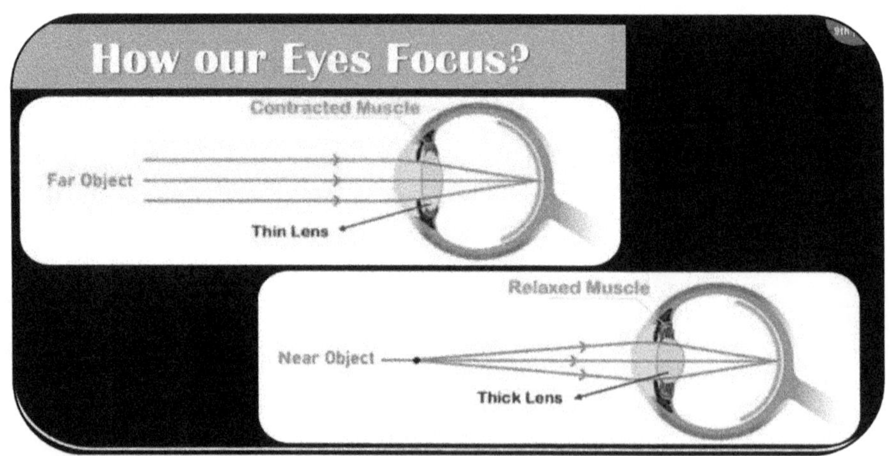

Defects of EYE

01. Myopia (near sightedness)

A myopic person can see nearby objects clearly but cannot see distant objects clearly. Image is formed in front of Retina.

Causes of Myopia -

- Excessive curvature of eye lens
- Stretching of eye ball

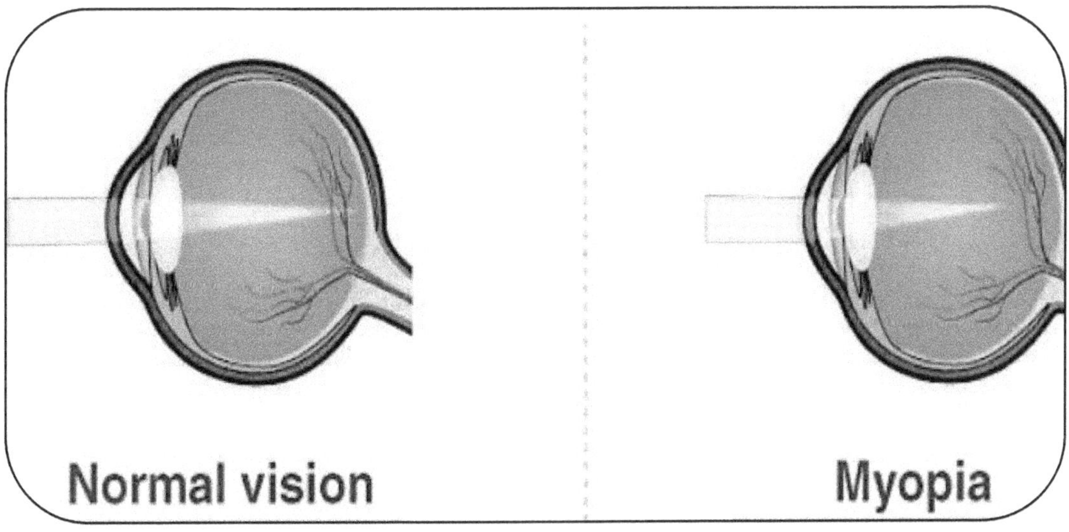

Correction

It is done by using concave lens of appropriate power.a) In a myopic eye, image of distant object is formed in front of the retina (not on retina)

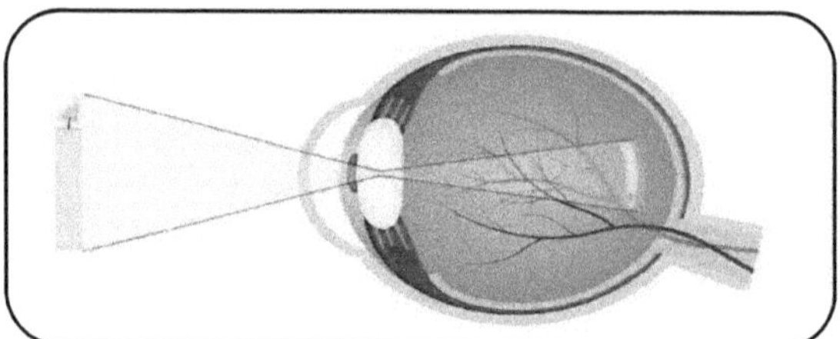

Correction

The far point (F) of a myopic eye is less than infinity.

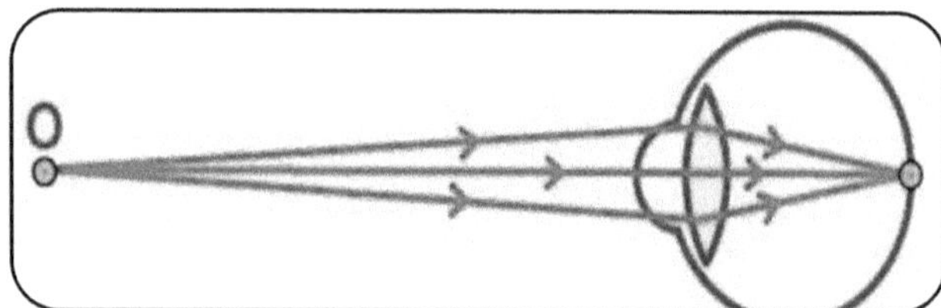

Correction

The concave lens placed in front of eye forms a virtual image of distant object at far point (F) of the myopic eye.

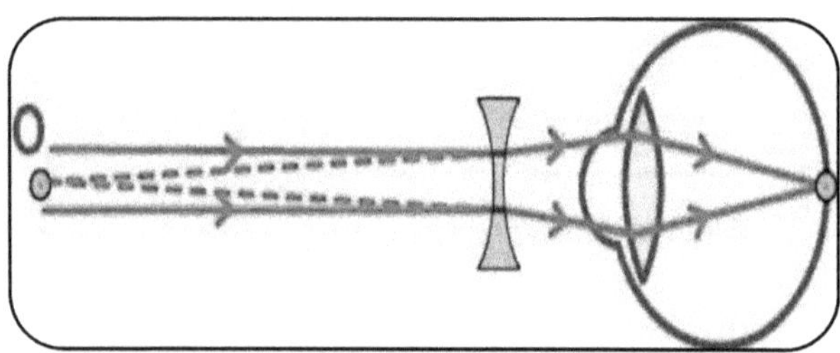

Hypermetropia (far sightedness)

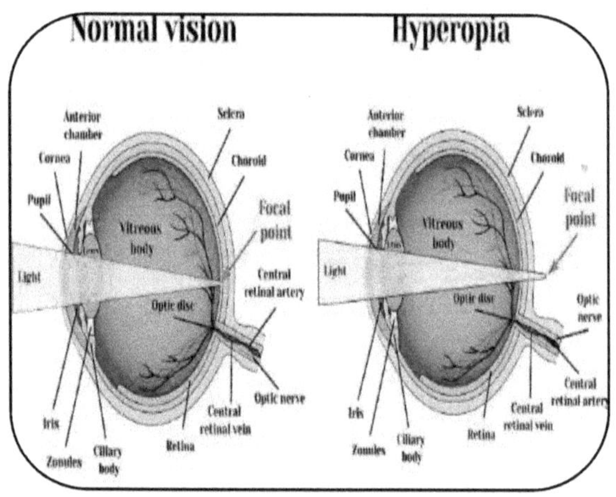

Affected person can see far objects clearly but can't see nearby objects clearly.

The near point of eye moves away.

Image is formed behind the retina.

Causes of Hypermetropia -

Focal length of eye lens becomes too long.

Eye ball becomes too small.

Correction

It is done by using convex lens of appropriate power.a) In a hypermetropic eye, image of distant object is formed behind the retina (not on retina)

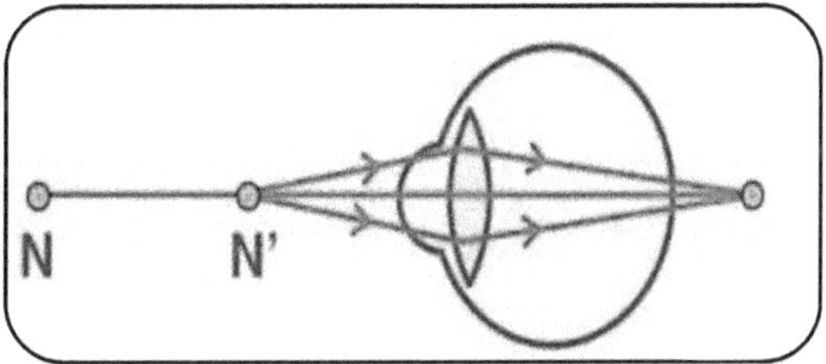

Correction

The near point (N) of a hypermetropic eye is more than 25cm

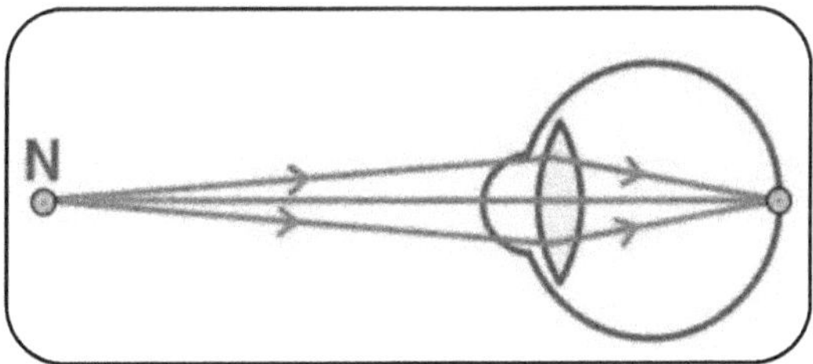

Correction

Correction of hypermetropia. The convex lens placed in front of eye forms a real image of near object on Retina.

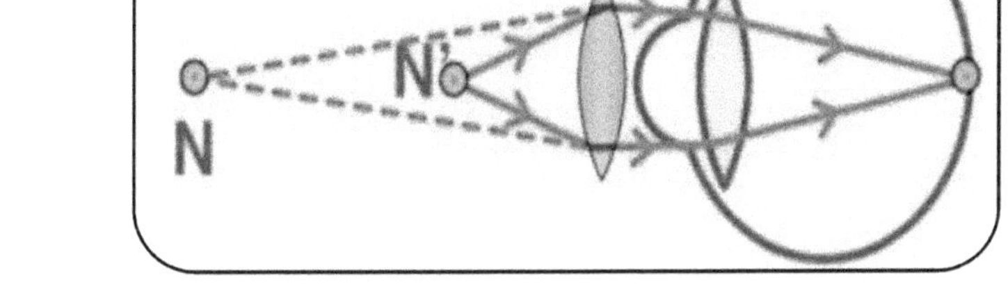

Dispersion of Light

The splitting of white light into its components due to different bending ability for colors when it passes through a prism is called DISPERSION OF LIGHT.

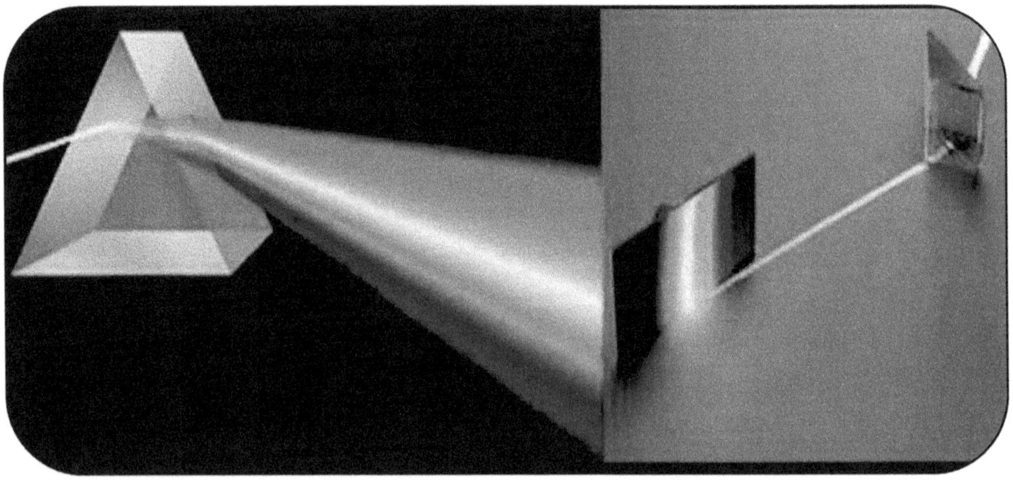

Total Internal Reflection

When light travels from denser medium to rarer medium with angle of incidence greater than critical angle then the refracted ray instead of emerging out again goes into the same medium. This is known as total internal reflection.

Two conditions:

i.   light travels from denser medium to rarer medium
ii.   ii. the angle of incidence is greater than critical angle

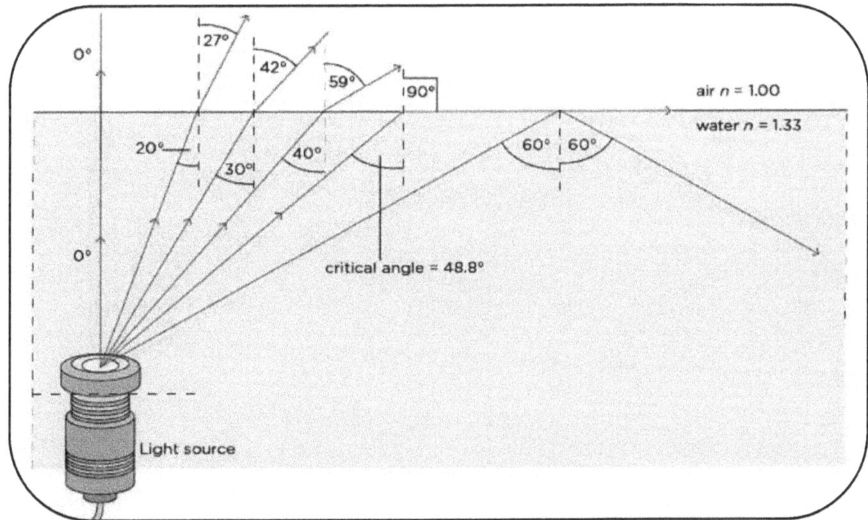

HOW A RAINBOW FORMS

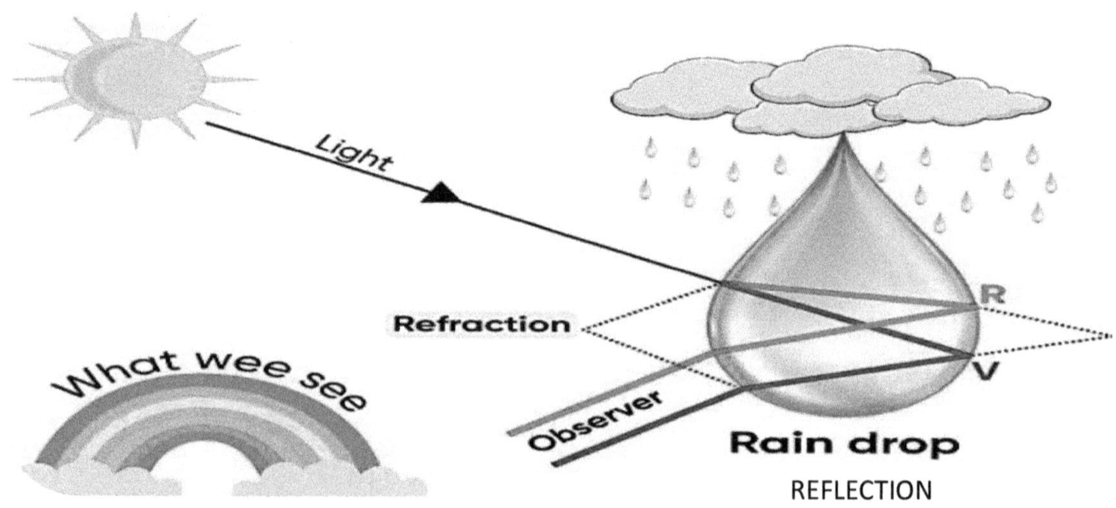

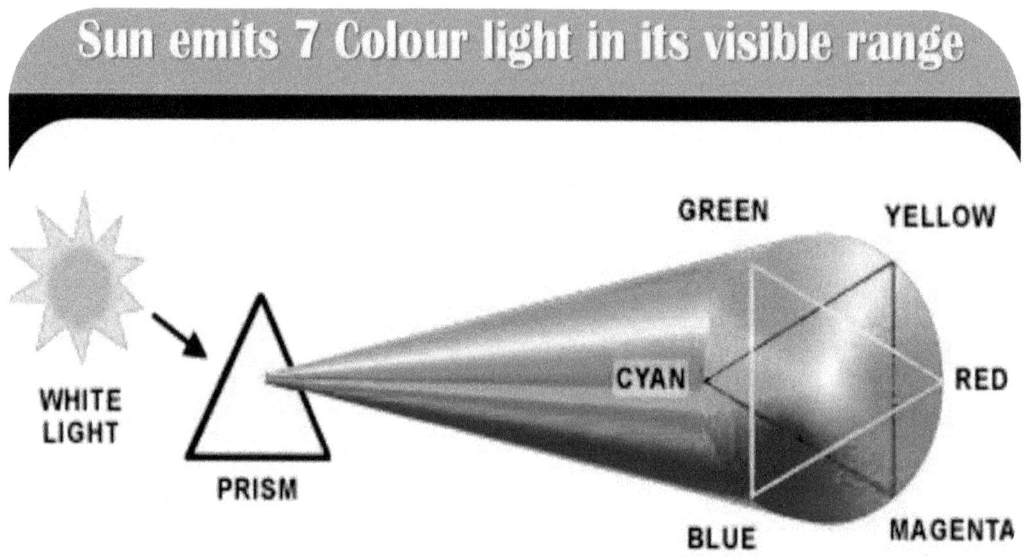

Blue Light is scattered more than other colors because it has shorter wavelength. Tiny atmospheric particles can scatter only shorter wavelengths.

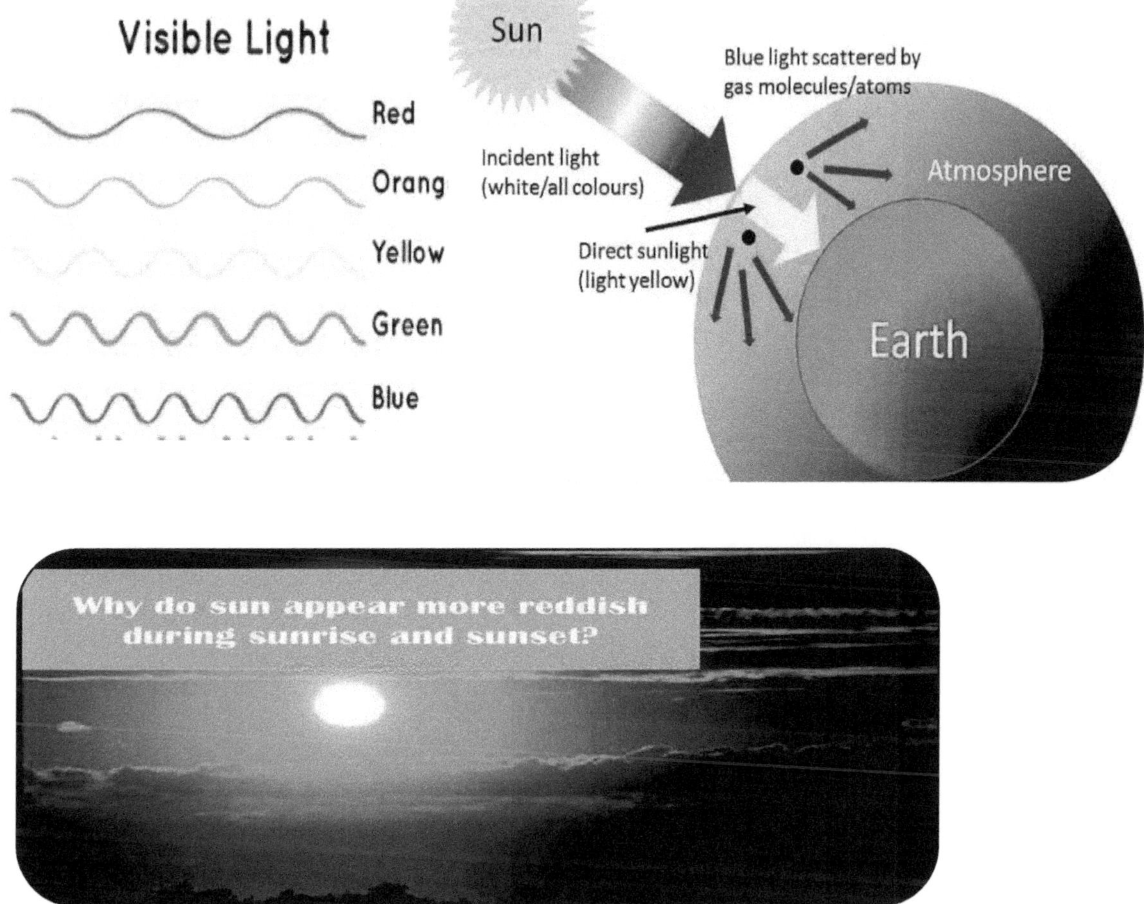

Light rays have to travel a larger part of the atmosphere because they are very close to the horizon. Therefore, light other than red is mostly scattered away.

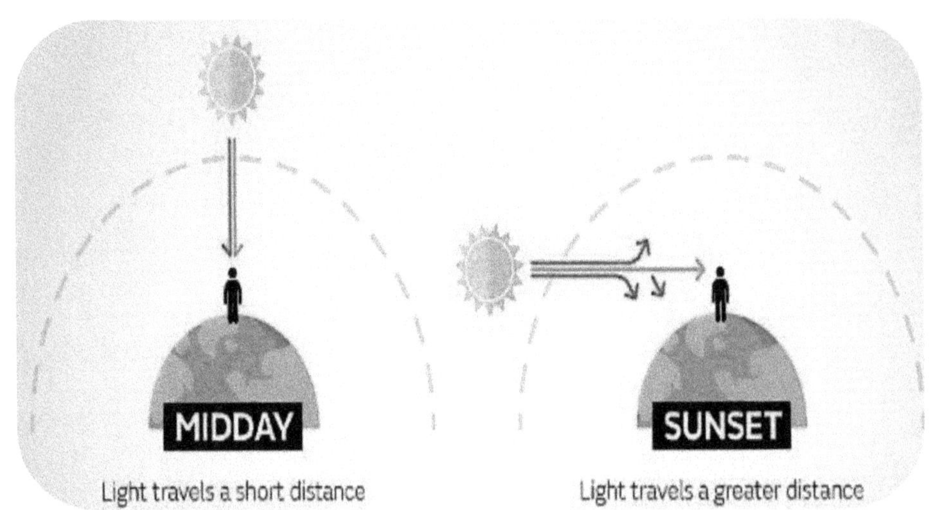

MIDDAY
SUNSET
Light travels a short distance
Light travels a greater distance

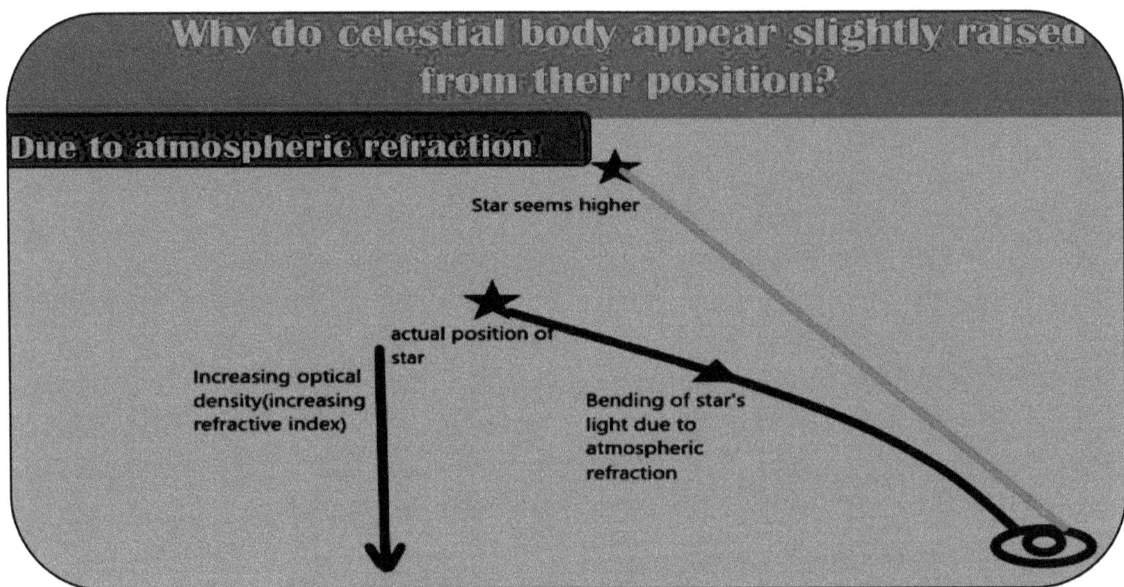

Why do celestial body appear slightly raised from their position?
Due to atmospheric refraction
Star seems higher
actual position of star
Increasing optical density(increasing refractive index)
Bending of star's light due to atmospheric refraction

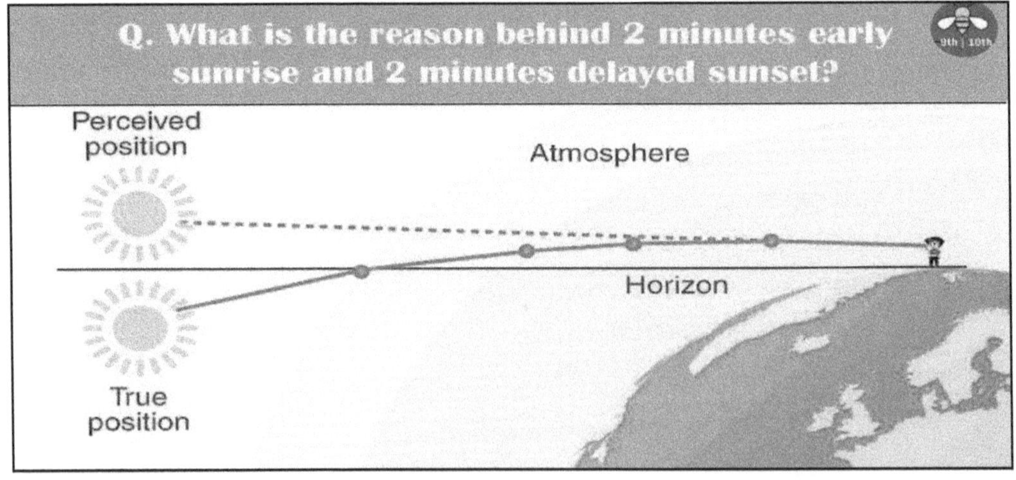

Q. What is the reason behind 2 minutes early sunrise and 2 minutes delayed sunset?
9th | 10th
Perceived position
Atmosphere
Horizon
True position

ANS : It is because of atmospheric refraction. When the star is slightly below the horizon, the light coming from it travels from less dense to more dense air and is refracted downwards.

Stars twinkle because of turbulence in the atmosphere of the Earth. As the atmosphere churns, the light from the star is refracted in different directions. Planets do not twinkle because they are not very far away from us like stars9h 10h.

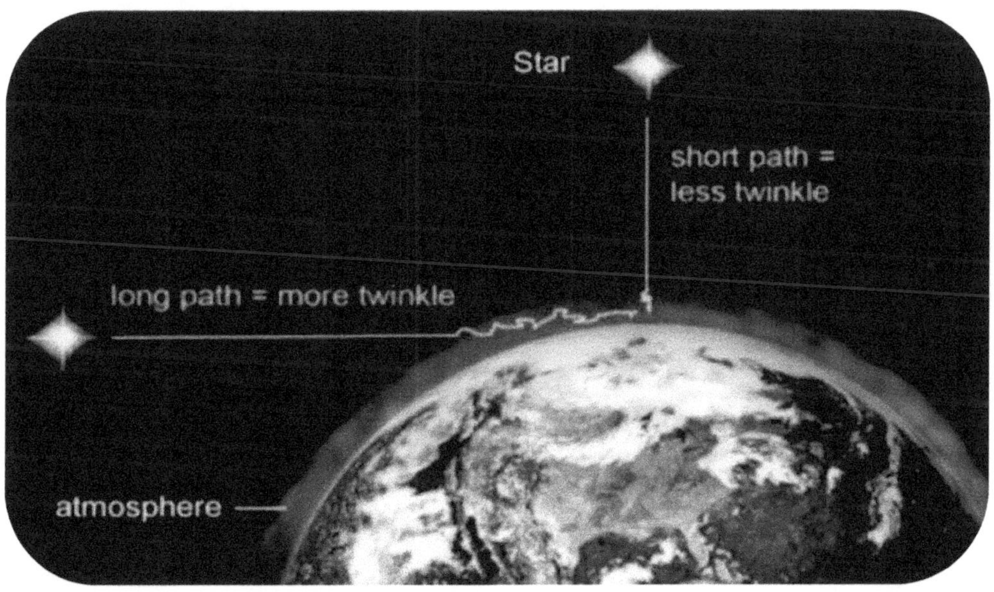

Electricity

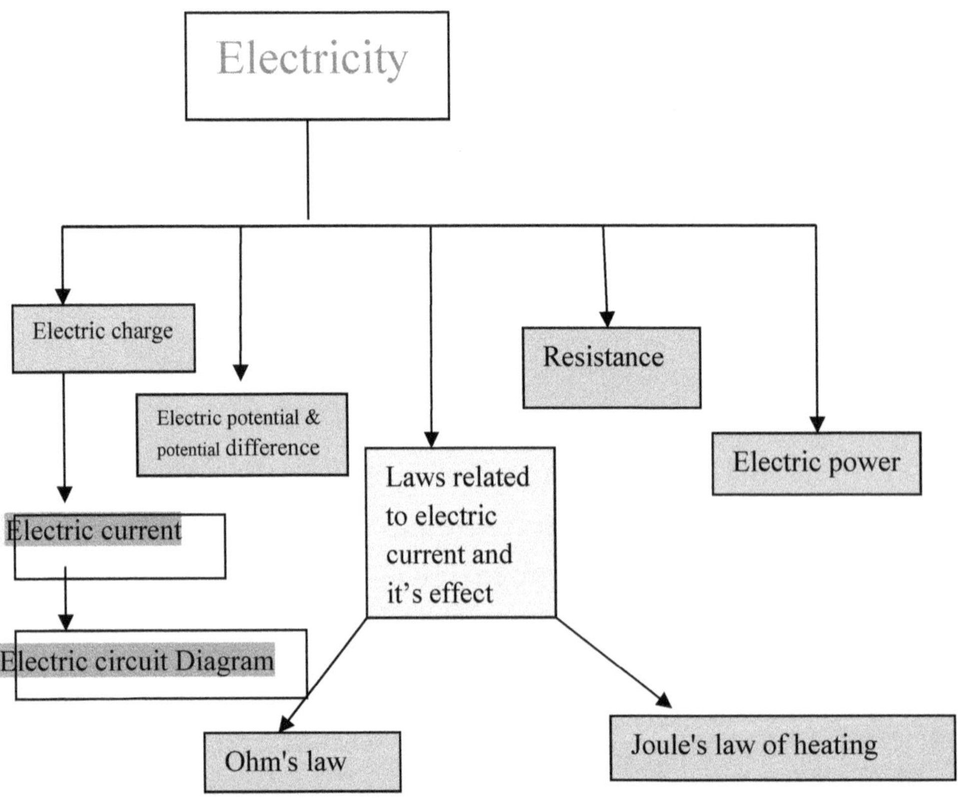

Conductors	Semiconductors	Insulators
Allow Current to pass	Medium Conductivity	Don't allow Current to pass

Electric Charge

Physical property of matter that causes it to experience a force when placed in an electromagnetic field.

S.I. Unit: Coulomb (C)

Positive charge : 

Negative charge : 

Loss of electron

Gain of electron

Properties:

1. Additivity of Charge : Total charge = sum of all charges on the body.

2. Charge is Conserved : Charge cannot be created or destroyed.

3. Charge is Invariant : Charge value remains the same, regardless of speed.

4. Quantization of Charge : Charge is a multiple of electron charge:

$$Q = ne$$

$$e = 1.6 \times 10^{-19} \text{ C}$$

For a material to be a good conductor of electricity, it must have free charge carriers like electrons or ions that can move freely within it.

STUDY OF CHARGE= ELECTRICITY

THE STUDY OF STATIC CHARGE = STATIC ELECTERCITY(ELECTROSTATICS)

STUDY OF DYNAMIC CHARGE = CURRENT ELECTERICTY(ELECTRODYNAMICS)

Electric Current = THE FLOW OF CHARGES IN A PARTICULAR DIRECTION (-VE TO +VE)

Unit: Ampere (A) 1 A = 1 C/s.

$$I = Q/t$$

I = current, Q = charge, t = time.

1 Ampere: When 1C of charge flows in 1 second then current is said to be 1A.

•**Ammeter: Measures and shows the intensity of electric current.**

•**Milliammeter: Measures small electric currents.**

•**Galvanometer: Detects and measures tiny electric currents.**

•**Voltmeter: Measures electric potential difference between two points in a circuit**

Potential Difference The work done to move a unit positive charge between two points.

Unit: Volt (V) 1 V = 1 J/C.

V = W/Q

1 Volt: Joule of work done to move 1 unit positive charge between two points.

Type of Questions asked ?

Step 1: Firstly check what question is asking and write given, to find from question.Out of V, W, Q two quantities will be given and you'll have to find third one.Also you might need to find out Q from the formulas:

I = Q/t or through Q = ne

Step 2: Then use the give formula to find unknowns:

V = W/Q

Don't forget to write units

Electric Circuit An electric circuit is defined as a continuous path

for current flow, consisting of a power source, conductor, and load.

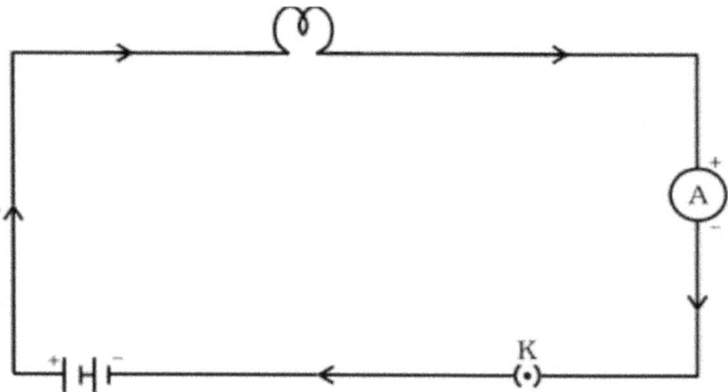

Electronic Circuit Symbols

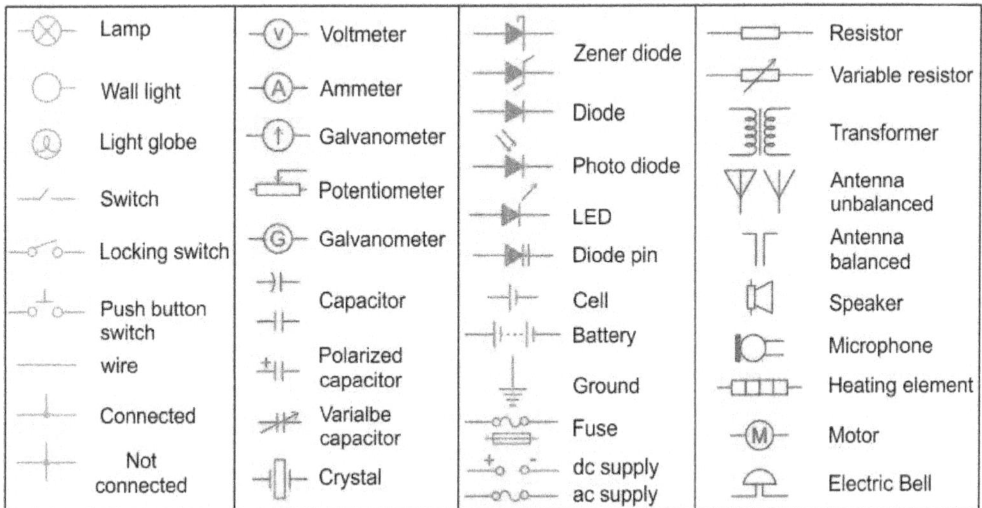

Symbol	Name	Symbol	Name	Symbol	Name	Symbol	Name
	Lamp		Voltmeter		Zener diode		Resistor
	Wall light		Ammeter		Diode		Variable resistor
	Light globe		Galvanometer		Photo diode		Transformer
	Switch		Potentiometer		LED		Antenna unbalanced
	Locking switch		Galvanometer		Diode pin		Antenna balanced
	Push button switch		Capacitor		Cell		Speaker
	wire		Polarized capacitor		Battery		Microphone
	Connected		Varialbe capacitor		Ground		Heating element
	Not connected		Crystal		Fuse		Motor
					dc supply		Electric Bell
					ac supply		

A schematic diagram is also shown, depicting a simple circuit with a cell, electric bulb, ammeter, and plug key.

Ohms Law

Definition:

Ohm's Law states the current through a conductor is proportional to voltage across it and inversely proportional to resistance.

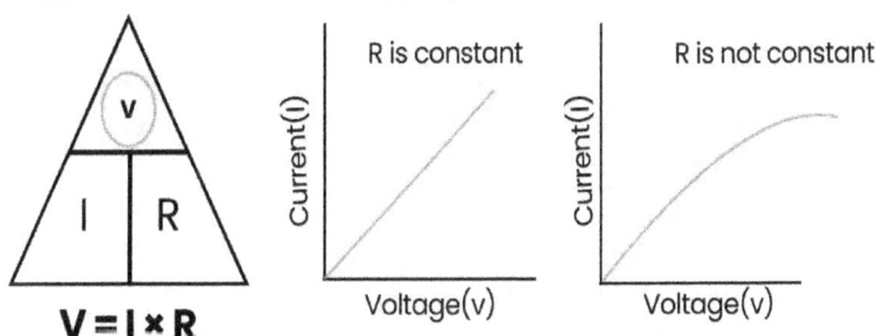

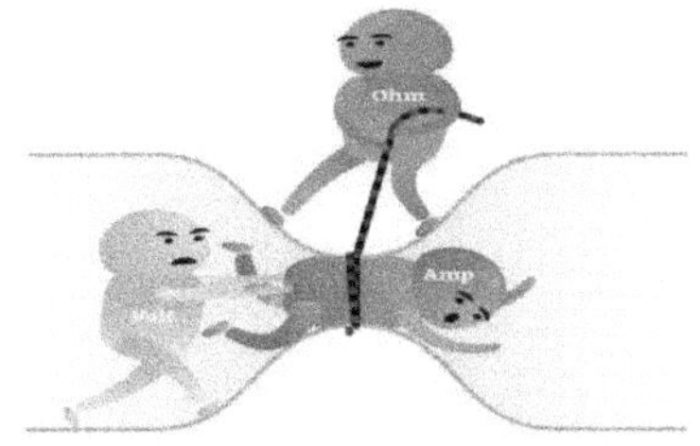

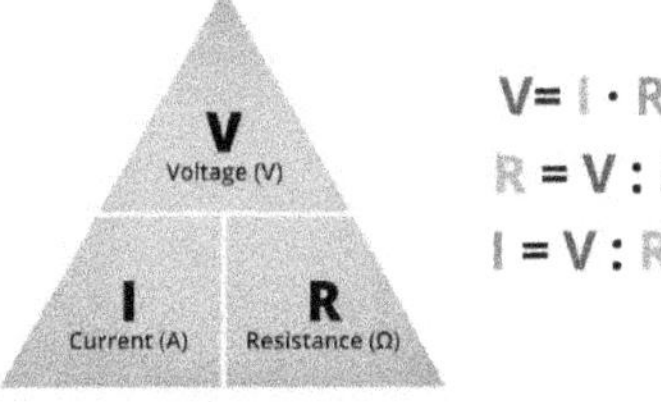

Resistance

Resistance is the property of a conductor that resists the flow of charges, measured in ohms.

The factors affecting resistance include:

Length (l): Resistance is directly proportional to length ((R \propto l)).

Area (A): Resistance is inversely proportional to the cross-sectional area ((R \propto 1/A)).

Material: Different materials have different resistivities ((\rho)).

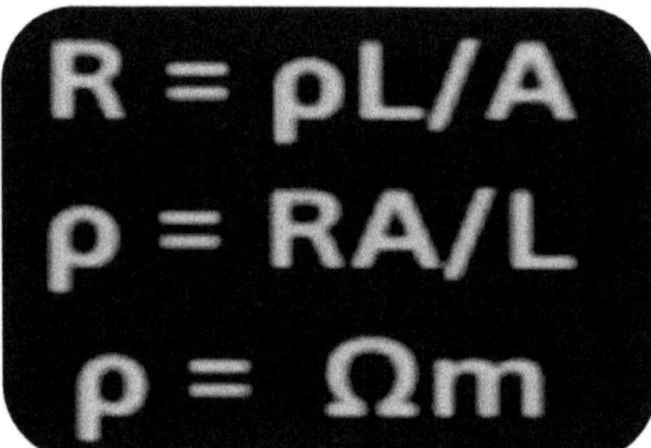

Resistance

- **These factors can be placed together to find resistance**

$$R = \rho l / A$$

Where R = resistance in ohms (Ω)

ρ = resistivity in ohm meter (Ωm)

l = length of wire (m)

A = cross-sectional area in meter square (m^2)

Resistance	Resistivity
Opposition to the flow of electric current in a substance	Resistance of a material with unit length and unit cross-sectional area
Extrinsic property	Intrinsic property
Depends on length and size of the conductor	Independent of length or size of the conductor
Unit: ohm (Ω)	Unit: ohm-meter ($\Omega{\cdot}m$)

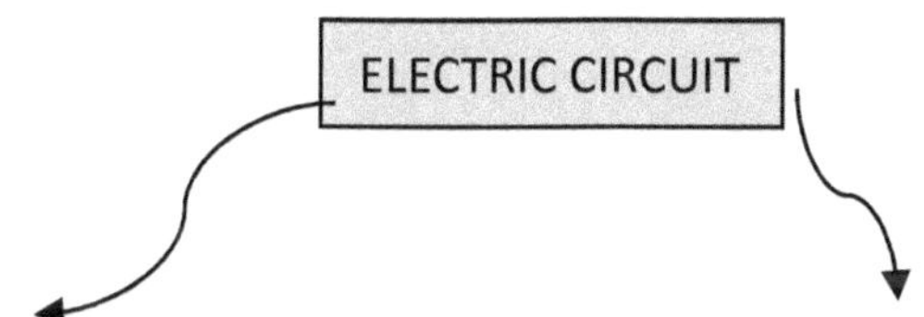

Series Circuit	Parallel Circuit
Current remains the same through all resistors	Current divides inversely proportional to resistance
Voltage divides across resistors based on resistance	Voltage remains the same across all resistors

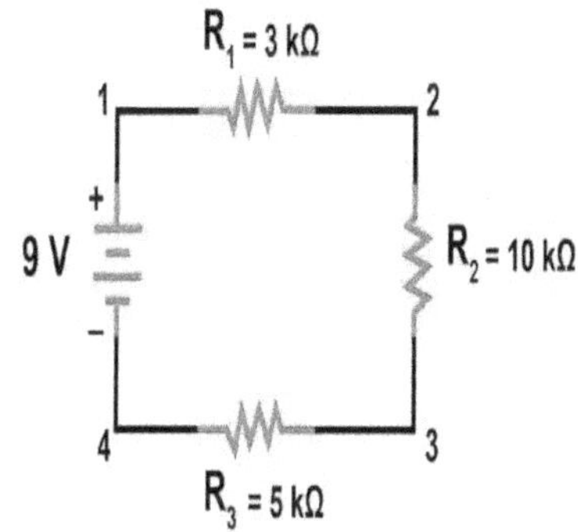

Series circuit with a battery and three resistors.

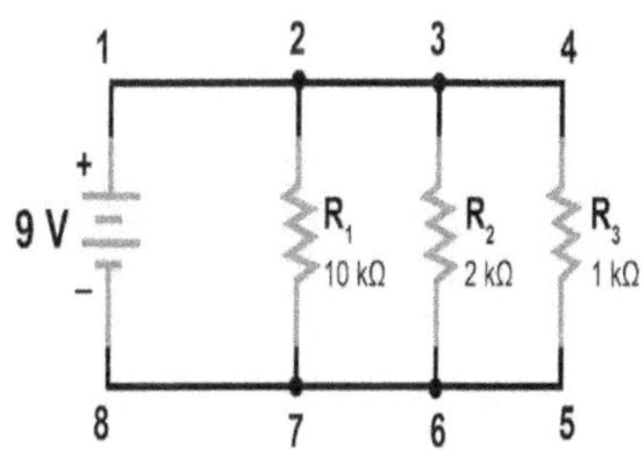

Parallel circuit with a battery and three resistors.

Derivations

Series Circuit	Parallel Circuit
Voltage: Total voltage (V) is the sum of the voltages across each resistor: $V = V_1 + V_2 + V_3$	Current: Total current (I) is the sum of the current through each resistor: $I = I_1 + I_2 + I_3$
Current: Current (I) is the same through each resistor.	Voltage: Voltage (V) is the same across each resistor.
Ohm's Law for Each Resistor: $V_1 = I\,R_1$, $V_2 = I\,R_2$, $V_3 = I\,R_3$	Ohm's Law for Each Resistor: $I_1 = V/R_1$, $I_2 = V/R_2$, $I_3 = V/R_3$
Equivalent Resistance: $V = I\,R$	Equivalent Resistance: $I = V/R_p$
Substituting: $I\,R = I\,R_1 + I\,R_2 + I\,R_3$	Substituting: $V/R_p = V/R_1 + V/R_2 + V/R_3$
Cancelling I: $R_s = R_1 + R_2 + R_3$	Cancelling V: $1/R_p \, 1/R_1 + 1/R_2 + 1/R_3$

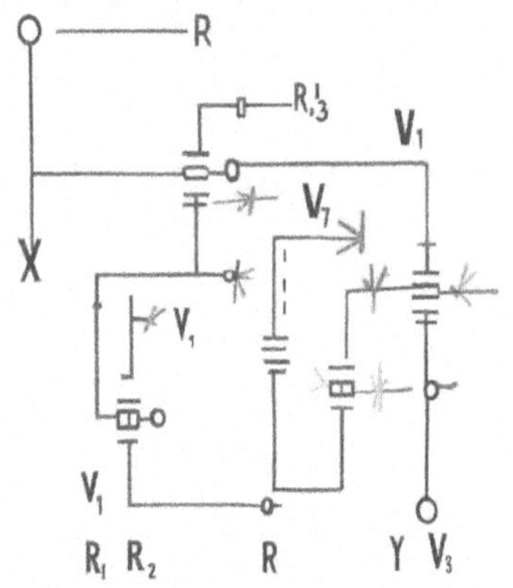

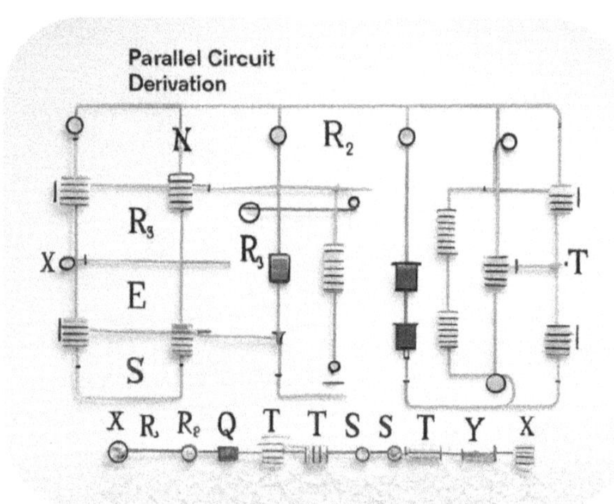

- Joules Law of Heating: Heat is proportional to the square of the current, resistance, and time.

For a current I flowing through a resistor of resistance R with a potential difference V, the work done to move a charge Q across the resistor is VQ. The power input to the circuit is:

$P = VQ / t = VI$

The energy supplied by the source in time t is VIt. This energy is dissipated as heat in the resistor, so the heat produced is:

$$H = VIt$$

Using Ohm's law, $V = IR$, the heat can also be expressed as:

$$H = I^2Rt$$

Applications:

• Electric Bulb: has a tungsten filament inside a neutral gas or vacuum. When current passes through, the filament heats up and emits light, with most energy lost as heat.

• Electric Fuse: is a low melting point wire in a circuit. If current rises suddenly, the wire melts, breaking the circuit and preventing damage.

• Electric Heater: use a nichrome coil with high resistance to generate heat when current flows.

Electric Power : **Power (P): Rate of energy consumption.**

Unit: Watt (W) 1W = 1 J/s.

$$P = VI$$

$$P = I^2R = V^2/R$$

1 watt is the power consumed by a device carrying 1A of current at 1V. In practice, a larger unit, the kilowatt (1000 watts), is used.

Electric Energy: *energy used by a circuit to allow current flow. It is the product of power and time, measured in watt-hours (Wh).*

Commercial Unit of Energy :One watt-hour is the energy used when 1 watt of power is consumed for 1 hour. The commercial unit of electric energy is the kilowatt-hour (kWh), also called a "unit".

1 kWh = 1000 watts x 3600 seconds

$= 3.6 \times 10^6$ watt-seconds

$= 3.6 \times 10^6$ joules (J)

Magnetic Effects of Electric Current

Magnetism in Nature

Moving Charges (Electric Current): Observed in solenoids, motors, etc.

Magnetisation: Iron, Nickel, Cobalt, and alloys can be magnetised.

Earth's Magnetism: Caused by the motion of ions and charges in Earth's core.

Hans Christian Oersted (1820): Discovered that electric current deflects a compass needle, proving the link between electricity and magnetism.

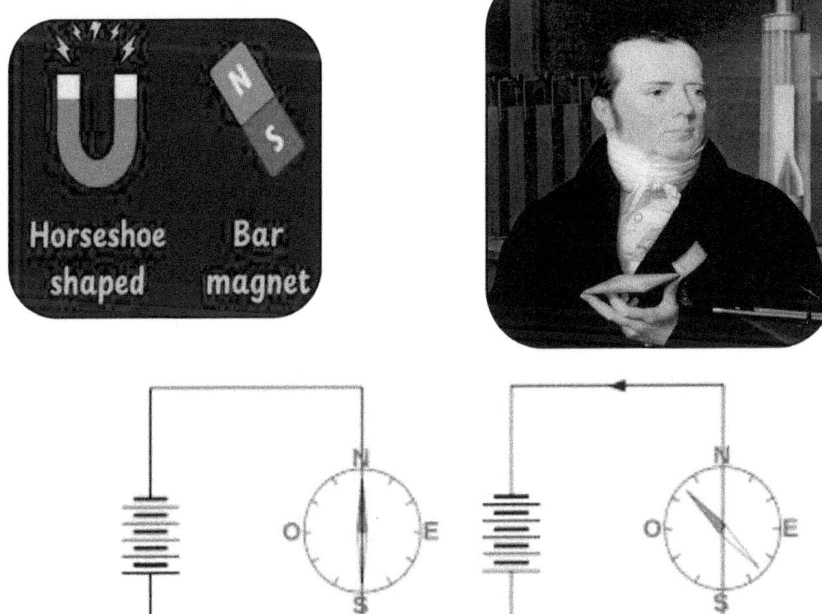

Magnet: A magnet is any substance that attracts iron or iron-like substances.

Properties of Bar Magnet:

•A freely suspended bar magnet aligns in

the Earth's north-south direction.

•Attractive and Repulsive Forces: Like poles

repel, opposite poles attract.

•Dipole Nature: Always has two poles (north and south); cutting the magnet creates smaller magnets, each with two poles.

•Creates a magnetic field around it where its effect can be felt.

•It retains its magnetic properties over time.

Magnetic Field: The area around a magnet in which the effect of magnetism is felt.

Magnetic Field Lines: Imaginary lines that show the strength and direction of a magnetic field.

Properties of Magnetic Field Lines:

•Magnetic field lines start at the north pole and end at the south pole.

•Closer lines mean a stronger magnetic field (near poles).

•Field lines never cross each other.

•They form closed continuous curves.

•They show the direction of magnetic force.

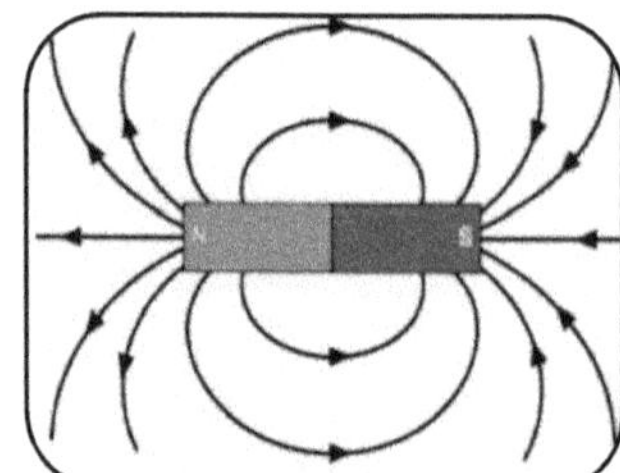

Maxwell's Right Hand Thumb Rule

The rule states that if a straight conductor carrying current is held in the right hand such that the thumb is pointed in the direction of the current, then the direction in which your fingers encircle the wire gives the direction of the magnetic lines of force around the wire.

Thumb = upwards, curled fingers = magnetic field (clockwise), the field direction = anticlockwise.

Thumb = downwards, curled fingers = magnetic field (anticlockwise), the field direction = clockwise.

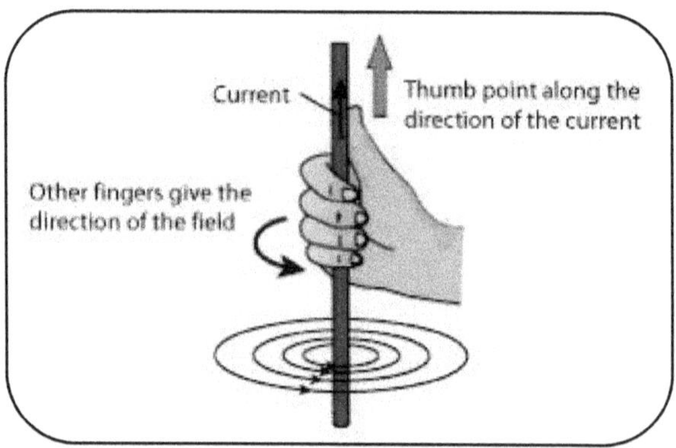

Magnetic field lines due to Straight conductor

01. Magnetic field lines form concentric circles with their centers on the conductor.

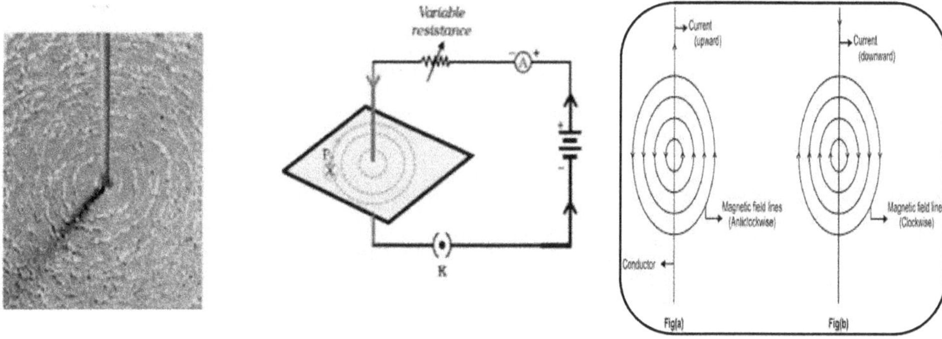

02. Magnetic field lines due to current carrying loop

- Circular pattern around the arms.

- Straight at the center of the loop.

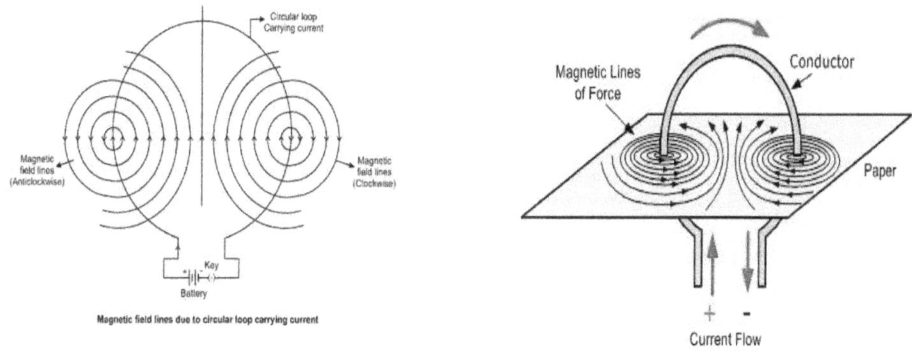

03. Magnetic field lines due to Solenoid

A coil of many circular turns of insulated copper wire wrapped closely in the shape of a cylinder.

Outside the solenoid: North to South

Inside the solenoid: South to North

Factors influencing the magnetic field

of a solenoid:

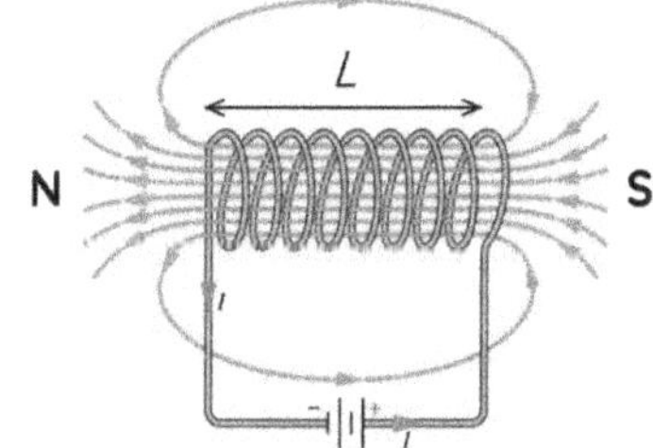

Number of turns in the coil,Amount of current flowing through it ,Radius of the coil , Material of the core of the solenoid

NOTE ; MEGNETIC FIELD DIRECTLY DEPENDS ON CURRENT

Electromagnet	Permanent Magnet
Works only when current flows	Always magnetic once magnetized
Strength changes with current	Strength depends on material
Loses magnetism when current stops	Loses magnetism permanently if demagnetized
Needs electricity to stay magnetic	No electricity required
Made of soft materials	Made of hard materials
Poles can switch with current	Poles stay the same

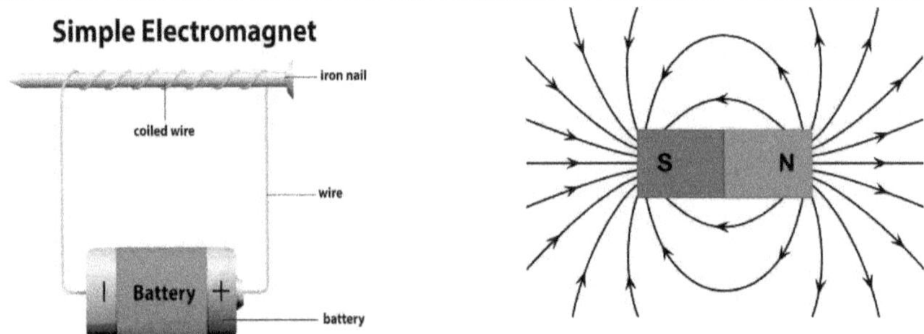

Force on a current carrying conductor in a magnetic field

Andre Marie Ampere's Suggestion: Magnet exerts equal and opposite force.

Force on a current-carrying conductor in a magnetic field.

Maximum displacement: When current is at a right angle to the magnetic field.

*Reversing current direction → Force direction is reversed.

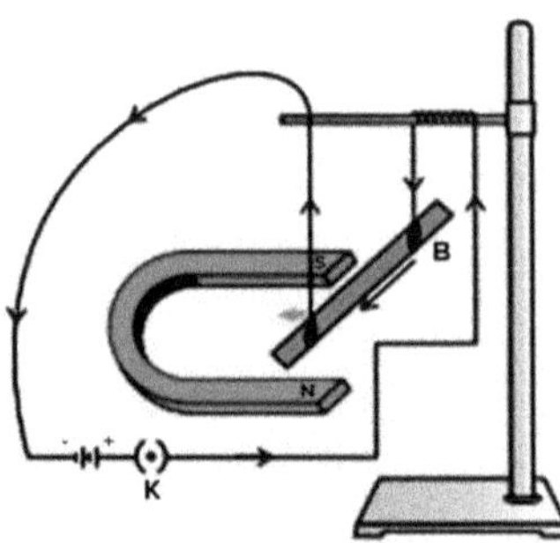

Fleming's Left Hand Rule

When a current-carrying conductor is placed in an external magnetic field, the conductor experiences a force that is mutually perpendicular to both the Magnetic field and the direction of the current flow.

Stretch the thumb, forefinger, and middle finger of your left hand perpendicular to each other.

Forefinger = Magnetic field direction

Middle finger = Current direction

Thumb = Force/motion direction

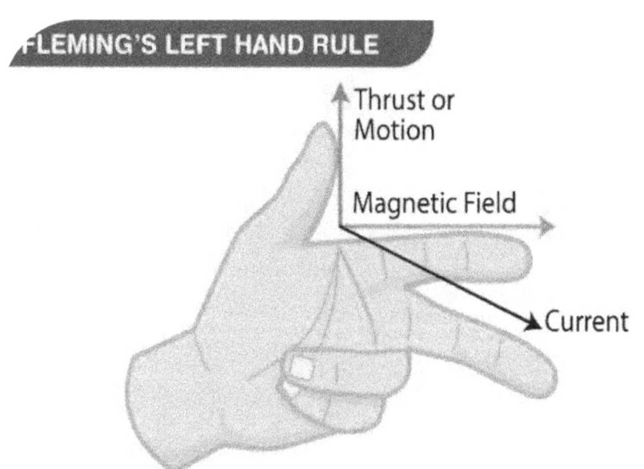

1/100 second in India, i.e., the frequency of A.C in India is 50 Hz.

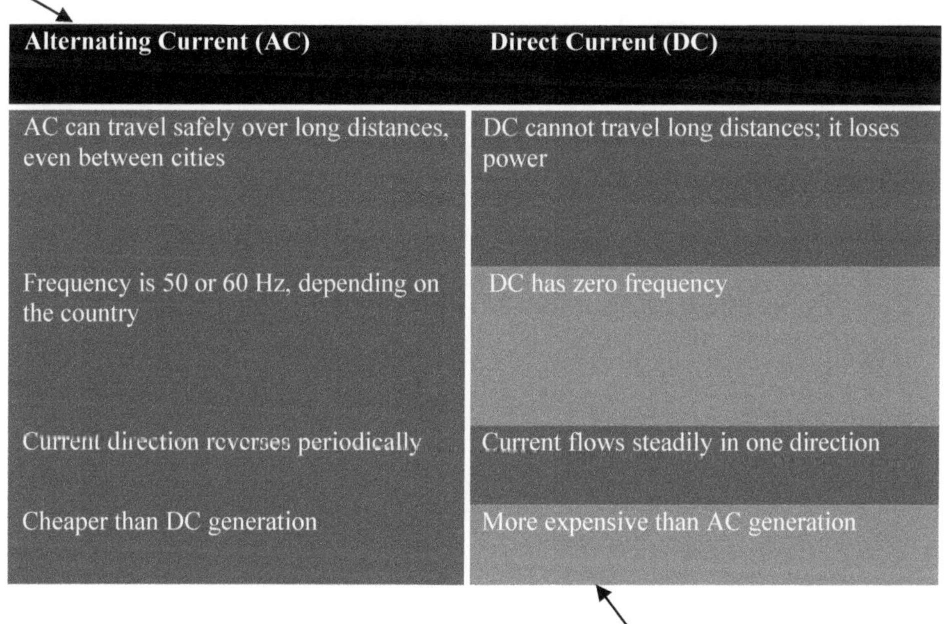

Alternating Current (AC)	Direct Current (DC)
AC can travel safely over long distances, even between cities	DC cannot travel long distances; it loses power
Frequency is 50 or 60 Hz, depending on the country	DC has zero frequency
Current direction reverses periodically	Current flows steadily in one direction
Cheaper than DC generation	More expensive than AC generation

Potential Difference in India: 220V at 50Hz.

WIRES IN DOMESTIC CIRCUITS

Earth Wire

•Generally green in color, connected to a metal plate in the earth as a safety measure.

•Grounds gadgets with metallic bodies, preventing shocks by grounding leaked charges.

Live Wire

•Positive, usually red, carries current in the circuit.

Neutral Wire

•Negative, usually black, returns electricity to the power source.

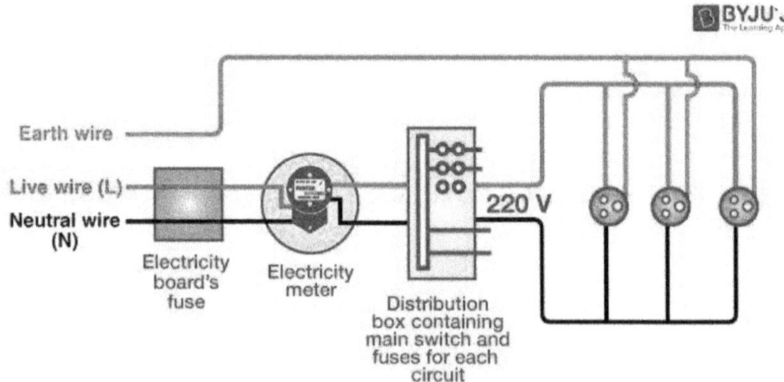

Domestic Electric Circuit

Sockets and Power Distribution

•Power sockets (15A): For high-power appliances (geyser, fridge, AC).

•Normal sockets (5A): For low-power appliances (TV, bulbs, fans).

Electrical Safety

Short Circuit

Occurs when a live wire and a neutral wire come into direct contact, causing a sudden and large amount of current to flow in the circuit.

• Reasons: Damage of insulation in power lines, fault in an electrical appliance.

Overloading

If the total current drawn through a wire by the appliances connected to it exceeds the safety limit for that wire, it gets overheated.

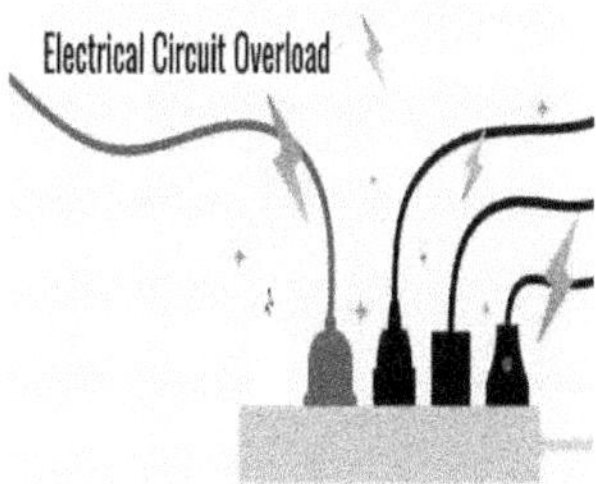

Electrical Fuse

A low melting point copper or other metal wire that breaks due to heat caused by overvoltage or high load to avoid short circuit or failure to the device.

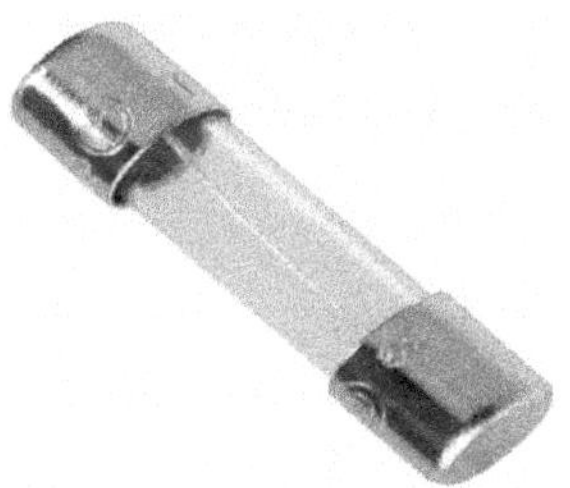

Chemistry

Faizan bhat

Chemical Reaction and Equation

Chemical Reaction The transformation of chemical substance into another chemical substance. e.g. Rusting of iron, the setting of milk into curd.

Chemical Equation:
Representation of chemical reaction using symbols and formulae of the substances

Make equations more informative:

- **Physical states** – solid (s), liquid (l), gas (g), aqueous solution (aq).
- **Concentration of acid** – Concentrated (conc.) Dilute (dil.)
- **Heat changes** –
  Reactant(s) → Product(s) + Heat
  Reactant(s) + Heat → Product(s)
- **Conditions to yield products**

Reactant(s)	(Temperature, Pressure, Catalyst	Product(s))
Reactant	Sunlight or hv	
Reactant	Heat or Δ	
Reactant	Electuds	

Zn (s) + 2HCl (aq, conc.) → (Heat) → ZnCl$_2$ (aq) + H$_2$ (g) + Heat

important terms:

- **Precipitate:** is the insoluble solid which settles down after the completion of the chemical reaction.
- **Exothermic reactions:** The chemical reactions that release heat energy.
- **Endothermic reactions:** The chemical reactions in which heat energy is absorbed.
- **Catalyst:** A catalyst is a substance that speeds up a chemical reaction, or lowers the temperature or pressure needed to start one, without itself being consumed during the reaction.
  e.g. Formation of ammonia (Haber's Process) – Fe (+ve catalyst)

Characteristics of Chemical Reaction:

i. Change in Colour	$Fe + CuSO_4$ (Blue) $\rightarrow FeSO_4$ (Blue-green) $+ Cu$
ii. Change in temperature	$CaO + H_2O \rightarrow Ca(OH)_2 + Heat$ *(heat is generated)*
iii. Change in State	$H_2(g) + O_2(g) \rightarrow H_2O(l)$ *(i.e. from gas to liquid)*
iv. Evolution of Gas:	$Zn(s) + H_2SO_4(aq) \rightarrow ZnSO_4(aq) + H_2(g)$
v. Formation of Precipitate	$Pb(NO_3)_2(aq) + KI(aq) \rightarrow PbI_2(s) + KNO_3(aq)$
vi. Endothermic reaction	$CaCO_3 + Heat \rightarrow CaO + CO_2$ *(photosynthesis also)*
vii. Exothermic reaction	$CaO + H_2O \rightarrow Ca(OH)_2 + Heat$ *(digestion and respiration also)*

Balanced Chemical Equation:

- Number of atoms of each element in reactants = number of atoms of each element in products
- Chemical equations are balnced in order to satisfy law of conservation of mass
- **Law of Conservation of Mass:** Mass of reactants = Mass of products
  "Mass is neither created nor destroyed in a chemical reaction."

Balance these:

$Fe + H_2O \rightarrow Fe_3O_4 + H_2$
$C_6H_{12}O_6 + O_2 \rightarrow CO_2 + H_2O$

$2H_2 + O_2 \rightarrow 2H_2O$: (Combustion of hydrogen)

$C_3H_8 + 5O_2 \rightarrow 3CO_2 + 4H_2O$: (Combustion of propane)

$Zn + 2HCl \rightarrow ZnCl_2 + H_2$: (Reaction of zinc with hydrochloric acid)

$Ca(OH)_2 + H_3PO_4 \rightarrow Ca_3(PO_4)_2 + 3H_2O$: (Neutralization reaction)

$Fe_2O_3 + 3CO \rightarrow 2Fe + 3CO_2$: (Reduction of iron oxide)

Types of Chemical Reactions:

1. Combination Reaction:

Two or more reactants combine to form single products.

$A + B \rightarrow AB$

Examples:
$$CaO + H_2O \rightarrow Ca(OH)_2$$
$$2H_2 + O_2 \rightarrow 2H_2O$$

Carbon dioxide Test:
The most effective way to test for CO_2 is to bubble the gas through lime water, which is a diluted solution of calcium hydroxide.

2. Decomposition Reaction:

A single reactant decomposes to form two or more products.

$$AB \rightarrow A + B$$

Examples:
$$CaCO_3(s) \rightarrow CaO(s) + CO_2$$
$$FeSO_4 \rightarrow Fe_2O_3 + SO_2 + SO_3$$

Decomposition Reaction

Thermal Decomposition

(initiated by thermal energy)
$$CaCO_3(s) \rightarrow (heat) \rightarrow CaO(s) + CO_2(g)$$
Calcium carbonate $\rightarrow$ Calcium oxide + Carbon dioxide

Photolytic Decomposition

(initiated by absorbing energy from photons)
$$2AgBr(s) \rightarrow (Sunlight) \rightarrow 2Ag(s) + Br_2(g)$$
Silver Bromide $\rightarrow$ Silver + Bromine
black and white photography

Electrolytic Decomposition

(initiated by electrical energy)
$$2H_2O(aq) \rightarrow 2H_2(g) + O_2(g)$$
Water $\rightarrow$ Hydrogen + Oxygen

Hydrogen (cathode) will produce a popping sound when a burning candle is brought close.
Oxygen (anode) will make the flame of the candle burn brighter.

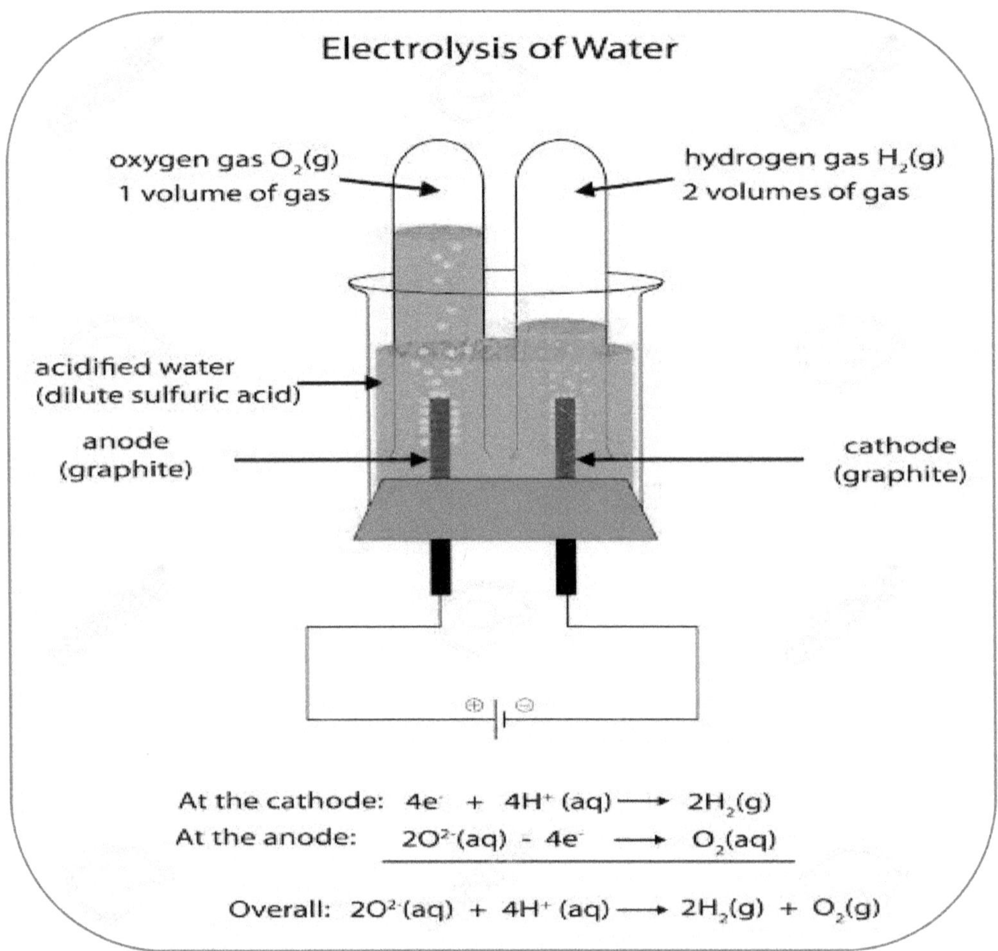

3. Displacement Reaction

Chemical reaction in which a more reactive element displaces a less reactive element from its compound.

Single Displacement

A + BC → AC + B
Zn + CuSO₄ → Cu + ZnSO₄

Double Displacement

AB + CD → AD + CB
Na₂SO₄(aq) + BaCl₂(aq) → BaSO₄(s) + 2NaCl(aq)

$$AB + CD \rightarrow AD + CB$$
$$Na_2SO_4(aq) + BaCl_2(aq) \rightarrow BaSO_4(s) + 2NaCl(aq)$$

Reactivity Series List of Metals arranged in order of their decreasing reactivity

Element Symbol	Element Name
K	Potassium
Na	Sodium
Ca	Calcium
Mg	Magnesium
Al	Aluminium
Zn	Zinc
Fe	Iron
Pb	Lead
H	Hydrogen
Cu	Copper
Hg	Mercury
Ag	Silver
Au	Gold

Most reactive (top)

Reactivity decreases ↓

Least reactive (bottom)

Trick = Katrina na car mangi alto zen farari phirbhi mile Hg ki Gadi

Chemical Reaction	Observation
$Mg + O_2 \rightarrow MgO$	Magnesium ribbon burns with a dazzling white flame and changes into a white powder (magnesium oxide).
Lead nitrate solution + Potassium iodide solution	A yellow precipitate of lead iodide forms, and the solution changes color from colorless to yellow.
Zinc granules + Sulfuric acid	Bubbles of hydrogen gas form around zinc. Reaction releases heat along with the gas.
$CaO + H_2O \rightarrow Ca(OH)_2$	Calcium oxide reacts vigorously with water, producing slaked lime and a large amount of heat.
$2FeSO_4 \rightarrow Fe_2O_3 + SO_2 + SO_3$	Originally green $\rightarrow$ turns white $\rightarrow$ then brown (ferric oxide) with a smell of burning sulfur.
Chemical Reaction / Activity	Observation
$2Pb(NO_3)_2(s) \rightarrow 2PbO(s) + 4NO_2 + O_2$	Brown fumes of nitrogen dioxide gas are released. Oxygen is also present. Yellow lead monoxide remains — appears reddish-brown when hot and yellow when cold.
$2AgCl(s) \rightarrow 2Ag(s) + Cl_2(g)$ (in sunlight)	White silver chloride turns grey in sunlight.
$Fe(s) + CuSO_4(aq) \rightarrow FeSO_4(aq) + Cu(s)$	Deep blue color of solution fades to light green, and iron nail becomes covered with a red-brown layer of copper.
$Na_2SO_4(aq) + BaCl_2(aq) \rightarrow BaSO_4(s) + 2NaCl(aq)$	A white precipitate will form.
$2Cu + O_2 \rightarrow 2CuO$	Forms a black substance (CuO). Hydrogen gas can be passed over the CuO causing a reverse reaction.

4. Redox Reactions: Oxidation + Reduction

- **Oxidation:** + oxygen or - hydrogen
- **Reduction:** - oxygen or + hydrogen

$$MnO_2 + 4HCl \rightarrow MnCl_2 + 2H_2O + Cl_2$$

Oxidizing agent:

An oxidizing agent is a substance that causes oxidation by accepting electrons; therefore, it gets reduced.

Reducing agent:

ZnO + C → Zn + CO

- ZnO is **Oxidised** (+O)
- C is **Reduced** (-O)

Effects of oxidation in daily life:

Corrosion:

Metals are gradually destroyed by chemical reactions with substances in their environment, such as moisture and acids.
Examples:
Rusting of iron, Tarnishing of silver, Green coating on copper.

Prevention:

Coating metals with protective layers (e.g., paint or galvanization) helps prevent direct exposure to oxygen and moisture, reducing the risk of corrosion.

Silver develops a black coating after some time.
$Ag + H_2S \longrightarrow Ag_2S + H_2$

Copper develops a green coating after some time.
$Cu + H_2O + CO_2 + O_2 \longrightarrow CuCO_3 \cdot Cu(OH)_2$

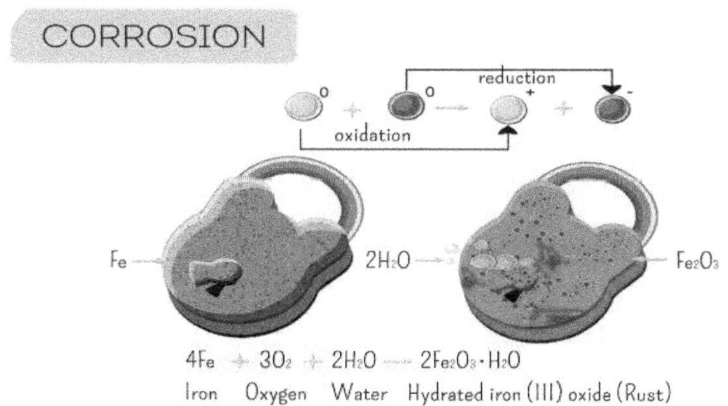

Rancidity:

The spoilage of fats and oils in food, leading to unpleasant taste and smell.
Examples: Spoiled butter, Old cooking oil, Stale chips.

Prevention:

Adding antioxidants, storing foods in airtight containers, and refrigerating can help slow down or prevent the oxidation process and, consequently, rancidity.

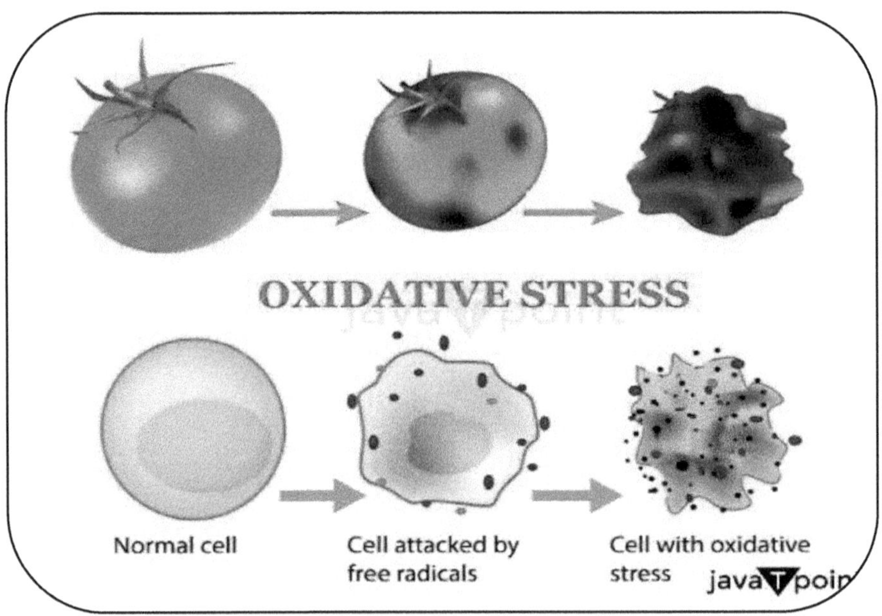

CARBON AND ITS COMPOUNDS

Carbon: Carbon is the 15th most abundant in the earth's crust.

- Atomic mass of C: 12u
- Valency of C: 4
- Atomic number: 6
- No. of protons = No. of neutrons = 6

Electronic Arrangement:
Shell – K L
No. of electrons – 2 4

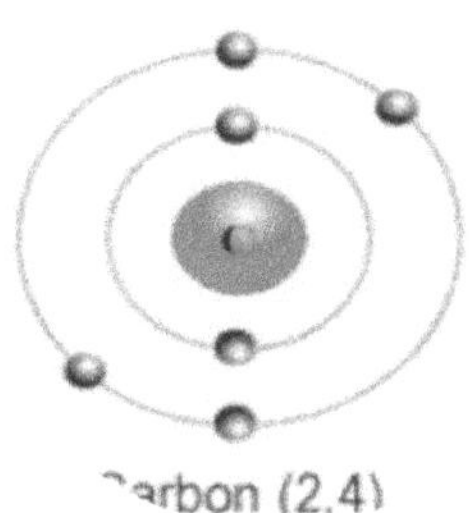

Covalent Bond:

A chemical bond that involves the sharing of electrons to form electron pairs between atoms.

- **Atomic Number of C: 6**
- **Electronic Configuration: 2 in first shell, 4 in valence shell**
- Achieve a stable (noble gas) configuration

   Gaining 4 electrons: Difficult to hold extra electrons

   Losing 4 electrons: Requires a lot of energy

- **Covalent Bonding:** C shares its valence electrons with other atoms

Three Types of Covalent Bonding:

1. **Single Covalent Bond** – H_2 molecule H–H
2. **Double Covalent Bond** – O_2 molecule O=O
3. **Triple Covalent Bond** – N_2 molecule N≡N

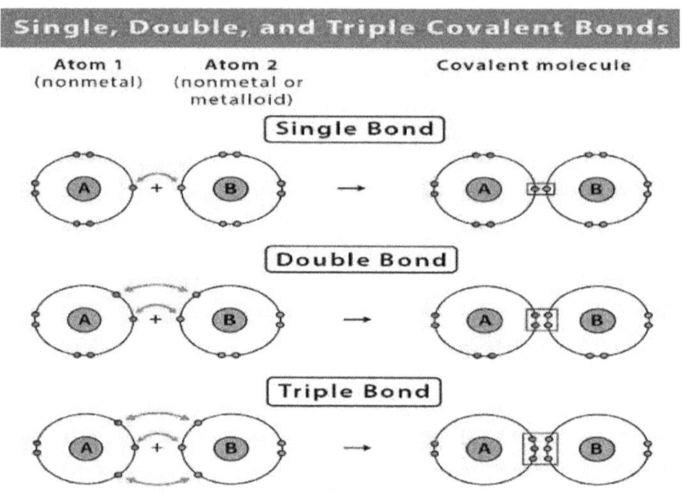

Properties of Covalent Compounds:

- Low melting/boiling points due to weaker intermolecular forces compared to ionic compounds.
- Physical state can be solid, liquid, or gas.
- Poor conductors of electricity as they lack charged particles.
- Generally **soluble in organic solvents, insoluble in water** (exception: sugar in water).

Tetravalency of Carbon:

Carbon has a valency of 4, allowing it to bond with elements like oxygen, hydrogen, nitrogen, sulfur, and chlorine. Its tetravalent nature means it needs four electrons to complete its outer shell.

Stability:

Carbon's small size allows its nucleus to hold shared electrons strongly, making carbon compounds generally stable.

Multiple Bond Formation:

Carbon can form single, double, and triple bonds with various elements.

Allotropes:

An element existing in the same physical state as other forms but with different chemical and physical properties.

Property	Diamond	Graphite	Fullerene
Structure	3D network, each carbon bonds with four others; very hard.	Layers of hexagons held by weak forces; soft and slippery.	Hollow, cage-like with 60 carbons; soccer ball shape.
Bonding	Four strong covalent bonds per carbon; highly stable.	Three covalent bonds per carbon, with delocalized electrons.	Strong covalent bonds in hexagons and pentagons.
Properties	Hard, transparent, high refractive index; jewelry, abrasives.	Soft, used in pencils and lubricants.	Unique electronic properties; used in nanotech, drugs.

HYDROCARBON

Compounds made up of H & C

Types of Hydrocarbons

1. Aliphatic Hydrocarbons

- **Saturated** – Single bond
  - o **ALKANES**:
    - Single bond between carbon atoms
    - *General formula:* C_nH_{2n+2}
- **Unsaturated** – Double or Triple bond
  - o **ALKENES**:
    - Double bond between carbon atoms
    - *General formula:* C_nH_{2n}
  - o **ALKYNES**:
    - Triple bond between carbon atoms
    - *General formula:* C_nH_{2n-2}

2. Aromatic Hydrocarbons

Intro to Saturated and Unsaturated Hydrocarbons

TYPES OF HYDROCARBONS

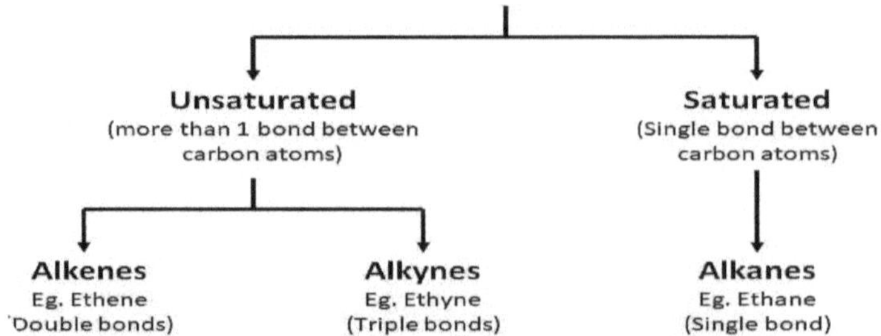

SATURATED → ALKANES

Name	Molecular Formula	Condensed Formula	Structural Formula
Methane	CH_4	CH_4	
Ethane	C_2H_6	CH_3CH_3	
Propane	C_3H_8	$CH_3CH_2CH_3$	
Butane	C_4H_{10}	$CH_3(CH_2)_2CH_3$	
Pentane	C_5H_{12}	$CH_3(CH_2)_3CH_3$	(similar pattern, extended chain)
Hexane	C_6H_{14}	$CH_3(CH_2)_4CH_3$	
Heptane	C_7H_{16}	$CH_3(CH_2)_5CH_3$	

ALKENE (Double Bonds)

Name	Molecular Formula	Structural Formula
Ethene	C_2H_4	$H_2C{=}CH_2$
Propene	C_3H_6	$CH_3{-}CH{=}CH_2$
Butene	C_4H_8	$CH_3{-}CH{=}CH{-}CH_3$ or other isomers

ALKYNE (Triple Bonds)

Name	Molecular Formula	Structural Formula
Ethyne	C_2H_2	$HC{\equiv}CH$
Propyne	C_3H_4	$CH_3{-}C{\equiv}CH$
Butyne	C_4H_6	$CH_3{-}C{\equiv}C{-}CH_3$ or isomers

Three Types of Hydrocarbons

1. Straight Chain Hydrocarbons

Each carbon atom is bonded to one or two other carbon atoms.
Examples:

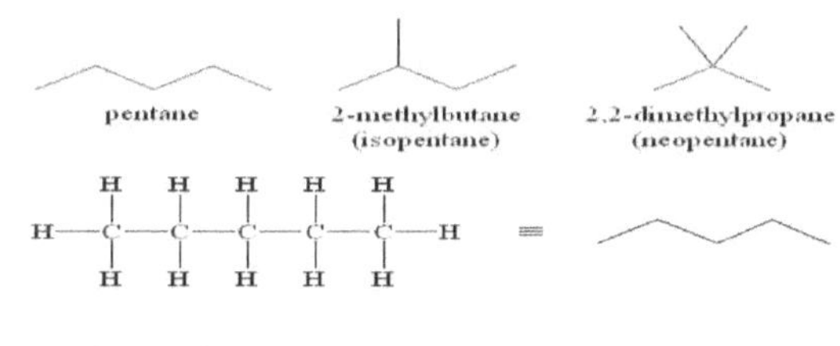

- Methane – CH_4
- Ethane – C_2H_6
- Propane – C_3H_8
- Butane – C_4H_{10}

(Structural examples shown as straight, continuous lines of carbon-hydrogen bonds.)

2. Branched Chain Hydrocarbons

Each carbon atom is bonded to one, two, or more than two other carbon atoms.
(Examples shown with central carbon branching out to more than two carbons.)

- **Saturated cyclic hydrocarbon**:
  - Cycloalkanes (C_nH_{2n})
- **Unsaturated cyclic hydrocarbon**:
  - Cycloalkenes (C_nH_{2n-2})
  - Cycloalkynes (C_nH_{2n-4})

cyclobutane   cyclopentane

Common Nomenclature

They are named after their sources of isolation.
Formic acid derives from **"Formectus"**, meaning red ant.
Acetic acid derives from **"Acetum"**, meaning vinegar.

International Union of Pure and Applied Chemistry (IUPAC), founded in 1919, establishes
standardized naming rules in chemistry.

ALKANES

IUPAC naming system:

Molecular formula	Condensed Structural Formula	Name
CH_4	CH_4	methane
C_2H_6	CH_3CH_3	ethane
C_3H_8	$CH_3CH_2CH_3$	propane
C_4H_{10}	$CH_3CH_2CH_2CH_3$	butane
C_5H_{12}	$CH_3CH_2CH_2CH_2CH_3$	pentane
C_6H_{14}	$CH_3CH_2CH_2CH_2CH_2CH_3$	hexane
C_7H_{16}	$CH_3CH_2CH_2CH_2CH_2CH_2CH_3$	heptane
C_8H_{18}	$CH_3CH_2CH_2CH_2CH_2CH_2CH_2CH_3$	octane
C_9H_{20}	$CH_3CH_2CH_2CH_2CH_2CH_2CH_2CH_2CH_3$	nonane
$C_{10}H_{22}$	$CH_3CH_2CH_2CH_2CH_2CH_2CH_2CH_2CH_2CH_3$	decane

Key Rules:

- **Longest Chain:** Choose the longest carbon chain.
- **Tie in Length:** Pick the chain with more substituents.
- **Numbering:** Number the chain to give substituents the lowest positions.
- **Naming Format:**
    - **Prefix + Root word + Suffix**

Prefixes:

Substituent names (e.g., methyl)

Root Word:

Based on the carbon chain length

Suffix:

- **"ane"** = single bond
- **"ene"** = double bond
- **"yne"** = triple bond

Additional Rules:

- For **alkenes/alkynes**, give the **lowest possible number** to double or triple bonds.
- **Same substituent:** Use **di-, tri-, etc.**
- **Number-letter format:** e.g., 2-methyl
- **Number, number format:** e.g., 2,2-dimethyl

Functional Groups

In hydrocarbons, hydrogen atoms can be replaced by heteroatoms (e.g., Cl, S, N, O), forming **functional groups** that determine the compound's reactivity and properties.

Rule I:

Choose the longest carbon chain with the functional group.

Rule II:

Number the chain to give the **lowest number** to the functional group (*First Locant Rule*). List substituents alphabetically.

Rule III:

Format: Prefix + Root Word + Primary Suffix + Secondary Suffix

Note: If a secondary suffix starts with **a, i, o, u, y**, omit the **"e"** in the primary suffix.

Functional Groups Table

Functional Group	Prefix/Suffix	Example & Formula
1. Halogen	Prefix – Chloro, Bromo, Iodo etc.	CH_3CH_2Cl – *Chloroethane*
2. Alcohol	Suffix – **ol**	CH_3CH_2OH – *Ethanol*
3. Aldehyde	Suffix – **al**	CH_3CHO – *Propanal*
4. Ketone	Suffix – **one**	CH_3COCH_3 – *Propanone*
5. Carboxylic Acid	Suffix – **oic acid**	CH_3COOH – *Ethanoic acid*
6. Alkyne	Suffix – **yne**	$CH{\equiv}CH$ – *Ethyne*, $CH_3C{\equiv}CH$ – *Propyne*

Characteristics:

- Share same general formula
- Differ by a -CH_2 group (mass difference of **14 μ**)
- Similar chemical properties
- Gradual change in physical properties
- Functional group influences properties

Isomerism

Compounds with identical molecular formula but different structures.

Example: **C_4H_{10}** can be:

- $CH_3-CH_2-CH_2-CH_3$ (Butane)
- $CH_3-CH(CH_3)-CH_3$ (Isobutane)

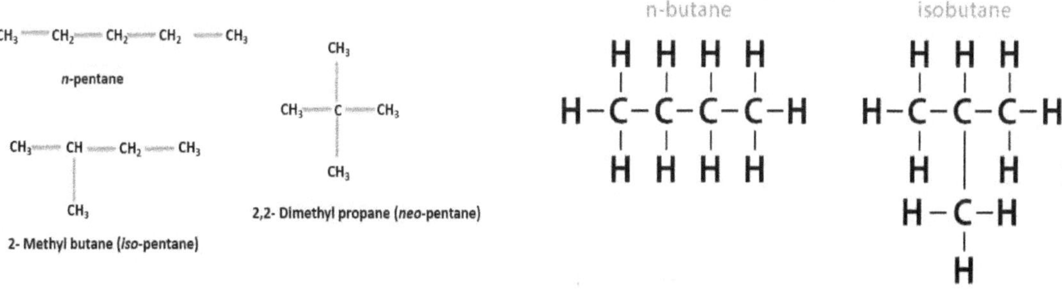

Chemical Properties of Carbon Compounds

Type of Reaction	Reaction	Observations
Combustion	(i) $C + O_2 \rightarrow CO_2$ + heat and light	Carbon burns in oxygen to release CO_2, heat, and light.
	(ii) $CH_4 + O_2 \rightarrow CO_2 + H_2O$ + heat and light	Methane combustion releases CO_2, H_2O, heat, and light.

	(iii) $CH_3CH_2OH + O_2 \rightarrow CO_2 +$ H_2O + heat and light	Ethanol combustion produces CO_2, H_2O, heat, and light.
Oxidation	$CH_3CH_2OH + [O] \rightarrow CH_3COOH$	Ethanol oxidizes to acetic acid using an oxidizing agent.
Addition Reaction	Unsaturated hydrocarbon + H_2 $\rightarrow$ Saturated hydrocarbon	Hydrogen adds to unsaturated hydrocarbons, used in hydrogenating oils.
Substitution Reaction	$CH_4 + Cl_2 \rightarrow CH_3Cl + HCl$ (in sunlight)	Chlorine replaces hydrogen in a fast substitution reaction.

Chemical Properties of Ethanol and Ethanoic Acid

Aspect	Ethanol (C_2H_5OH)	Ethanoic Acid (CH_3COOH)
Common Names	Alcohol, Ethyl Alcohol	Acetic Acid
Physical Properties	Liquid at room temp., soluble in water	Liquid, freezes at 290 K to form "glacial acetic acid"
Uses	Alcoholic drinks, medicines (tincture iodine, syrups), solvent	Used in vinegar (5–8% solution), preservative in pickles
Reaction with Sodium	$2Na + 2C_2H_5OH \rightarrow 2C_2H_5ONa + H_2$	No reaction
Dehydration Reaction	C_2H_5OH (hot conc. H_2SO_4 at 443 K) $\rightarrow CH_2=CH_2 + H_2O$ (forms ethene)	No reaction
Effect on Health	Drunkenness, impairs CNS; methanol is lethal; ethanol is denatured	Safe in vinegar amounts; weak acid
Esterification Reaction	$C_2H_5OH + CH_3COOH$ + conc. $H_2SO_4 \rightarrow CH_3COOC_2H_5 + H_2O$	Forms ester with ethanol in presence of conc. H_2SO_4
Saponification Reaction	Ester + NaOH $\rightarrow$ Alcohol + Sodium salt	Ester + NaOH $\rightarrow$ Alcohol + Sodium acetate
Reaction with Base	No reaction	$CH_3COOH + NaOH \rightarrow$ $CH_3COONa + H_2O$
Reaction with Carbonates & Bicarbonates	No reaction	$CH_3COOH + Na_2CO_3 \rightarrow$ $CH_3COONa + CO_2 + H_2O$ $CH_3COOH + NaHCO_3 \rightarrow$ $CH_3COONa + CO_2 + H_2O$ *(CO_2 testable with limewater)*

Esterification Reaction

Ethanoic acid reacts with ethanol in the presence of an acid catalyst (usually concentrated sulfuric acid) to form an ester and water.

Equation:

$CH_3COOH + C_2H_5OH$
(conc. H_2SO_4) $\rightarrow CH_3COOC_2H_5 + H_2O$

Saponification Reaction

When an ester reacts with sodium hydroxide, it produces an alcohol and a sodium salt of the carboxylic acid.

Equation:

$CH_3COOC_2H_5 + NaOH \rightarrow C_2H_5OH + CH_3COONa$

Cleansing Action of Soap/Detergent

1. **Soap molecules in water have a hydrophilic end and a hydrophobic tail.**
2. **At the water surface**, the hydrophobic tail aligns out of water, while the ionic end remains in water.
3. **In water**, hydrophobic tails orient away from water, leading to clustering.
4. **Micelles form** with hydrophobic tails clustered in the center and ionic ends on the surface.
5. **Oily dirt collects** inside the micelle's hydrophobic core.
6. **Micelles remain suspended** in solution due to ion-ion repulsion, preventing precipitation.
7. **Micelles with trapped dirt** are easily rinsed away.
8. **Micelle formation scatters light**, resulting in a cloudy appearance.

Illustration Note:

Soap molecule is labeled with:

- **Hydrophobic tail**
- **Hydrophilic head**

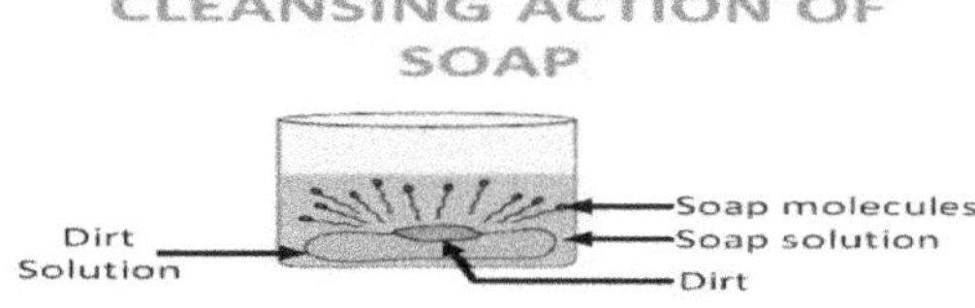

Soaps vs. Detergents

Aspect	Soap	Detergent
Chemical Composition	Sodium or potassium salts of long-chain carboxylic acids	Sodium salts of sulphonic acids or ammonium salts with chloride or bromide ions
Structure	Has a hydrophilic (water-attracting) ionic end and a hydrophobic (water-repelling) hydrocarbon tail	Similar structure with a hydrophilic head and hydrophobic tail
Formation of Micelles	Forms micelles in water, which trap dirt and oil inside	Also forms micelles in water, making it effective for cleaning
Effectiveness in Hard Water	Forms scum with calcium and magnesium ions in hard water, reducing cleaning efficiency	Does not form scum in hard water, remains effective
Foam Formation	Less foam in hard water, more in soft water	Produces foam even in hard water
Use in Cleaning	Commonly used for personal hygiene and in soft water	Used in laundry, shampoos, and hard water cleaning applications
Environmental Impact	Biodegradable, generally environmentally friendly	Some detergents are non-biodegradable, may contribute to water pollution
Cost	Usually cheaper than detergents	Often more expensive, especially those formulated for specific cleaning tasks

Metals and Non Metals

Elements (118)

Metals ((93)

e.g. Gold (Au), Iron (Fe), Zinc (Zn), Lead (Pb).

Non Metals (22)

e.g. Hydrogen (H), Helium (He), Oxygen (O).

Metalloids (07)

e.g. Boron (B), Silicon (Si), Germanium (Ge), Antimony (Sb).

Noble Gas

e.g. Helium (He), Neon (Ne), Argon (Ar).

Property Comparison: Metals vs Non Metals

Property	Metals	Non Metals
Malleability	Malleable (can be hammered). Ex: Aluminium, Iron. Exceptions: Zinc, Arsenic, Mercury.	Brittle (easily break). Ex: Sulphur, Phosphorus.
Ductility	Ductile (can be drawn into wires). Ex: Copper, Al. Exceptions: Mercury, Zinc.	Not ductile. Ex: Sulphur, Iodine.
Hardness	Mostly hard. Ex: Iron, Aluminium. Except - sodium and potassium.	Soft (except diamond).

More Properties

Property	Metals	Non Metals
Sonority	Sonorous (produces sound). Ex: Iron, Copper. Exceptions: Mercury.	Non-sonorous.
Lustre	Lustrous (shiny). Ex: Gold, Aluminium.	Dull (except iodine).
Melting/Boiling Point	High. Ex: Tungsten, Gold. Exceptions: Sodium, Potassium, Mercury, Gallium, Cesium.	Low (except diamond).
Electrical Conductivity	Good conductor. Ex: Silver, Copper. Exceptions: Mercury, Lead.	Poor conductor (except graphite).
Heat Conductivity	Good conductor. Ex: Silver, Copper. Exceptions: Mercury, Lead.	Poor conductor (except graphite).
State	Solid (except mercury).	Can be solid, liquid, or gas.
Density	High density. Ex: Gold, Iron.	Low density. Ex: Hydrogen, Nitrogen.

Interesting Facts:

- *Metals: Mercury is liquid at room temp. Gallium melts in hand.*
- *Non Metals: Graphite conducts electricity. Diamond is hardest.*

Reactions of Metals and Non-Metals

Reaction with	Metals	Non-Metals
Oxygen	**Metal + Oxygen → Metal Oxide (Basic)** **Example:** $2Mg + O_2 \rightarrow 2MgO$ **Amphoteric Metals:** Beryllium (Be), Zinc (Zn), Tin (Sn), Lead (Pb), Aluminium (Al), Antimony (Sb) **Reactions:** • Aluminium + Oxygen: $4Al(s) + 3O_2(g) \rightarrow 2Al_2O_3(s)$ • Zinc + Oxygen: $2Zn(s) + O_2(g) \rightarrow 2ZnO(s)$ **Aluminium Oxide Reactions:** 1. $Al_2O_3(s) + 6HCl(aq) \rightarrow 2AlCl_3(aq) + 3H_2O(l)$ 2. $Al_2O_3(s) + 2NaOH(aq) \rightarrow 2NaAlO_2(aq) + H_2O(l)$	**Non-Metal + Oxygen → Non-Metal Oxide (Acidic or Neutral)** **Examples:** • $C + O_2 \rightarrow CO_2$ • $S + O_2 \rightarrow SO_2$
Water	**Metal + Water → Metal Hydroxide + H_2** **Examples:** • $2Na + 2H_2O \rightarrow 2NaOH + H_2$ **Mildly reactive metals:** • $Ca + 2H_2O \rightarrow Ca(OH)_2 + H_2$	**Non-metals do not react with water** **However:** **Non-metal oxide + Water → Acid** • $SO_2 + H_2O \rightarrow H_2SO_3$ • $SO_3 + H_2O \rightarrow H_2SO_4$

	With steam: • $2Al + 3H_2O$ (steam) $\rightarrow Al_2O_3 + 3H_2$ • $3Fe + 4H_2O$ (steam) $\rightarrow Fe_3O_4 + 4H_2$ **Unreactive with water:** Pb, Cu, Ag, Au	• $CO_2 + H_2O \rightarrow H_2CO_3$ • $NO_2 + H_2O \rightarrow HNO_3 + HNO_2$

Reactions with Acids and Metal Salts

Reaction with	Metals	Non-Metals
Acids	**Metal + Dilute Acid $\rightarrow$ Salt + H$_2$** **Example**: $Zn + 2HCl \rightarrow ZnCl_2 + H_2$ **Note**: Hydrogen gas isn't produced when metals react with HNO_3 because it oxidizes H_2 to water and reduces to nitrogen oxides. Only Mg and Mn with very dilute HNO_3 release H_2 gas. **Reactions with Dilute Nitric Acid:** - **Mg**: $2Mg + 4HNO_3 \rightarrow 2Mg(NO_3)_2 + H_2$ - **Mn**: $Mn + 2HNO_3 \rightarrow Mn(NO_3)_2 + H_2$ **Other Metals**: Metal + Dilute $HNO_3 \rightarrow$ Salt + Water + $NO_2/NO/N_2O$ **Aqua Regia** (HNO_3:HCl = 1:3) is highly corrosive and can dissolve gold & platinum: **$HNO_3 + 3HCl \rightarrow NOCl + Cl_2 + 2H_2O$**	**No Reaction**
Metal Salts	**Displacement Reaction:** More reactive metals displace less reactive ones from their salt solutions. **Reaction:** Metal A + Salt solution of B $\rightarrow$ Salt solution of A + Metal B **Example:** $Pb + CuCl_2 \rightarrow PbCl_2 + Cu$	**No Reaction**

Reactivity Series of Metals

Symbol	Element	Reactivity
K	Potassium	Most reactive
Na	Sodium	
Ca	Calcium	
Mg	Magnesium	
Al	Aluminium	
Zn	Zinc	
Fe	Iron	Reactivity decreases
Pb	Lead	
H	Hydrogen	
Cu	Copper	
Hg	Mercury	

Ag	Silver	
Au	Gold	Least reactive

Reactions of Metals with Non-Metals (Ionic Bonding)

When metals react with non-metals, electrons transfer from metals to non-metals, forming ions. The compound formed is **ionic**.

General Reaction:

Metal + Non-metal → Ionic Compound

Example: Sodium and Chlorine

1. **Sodium (Na)** loses 1 electron → **Na$^+$** (cation)
2. **Chlorine (Cl)** gains 1 electron → **Cl$^-$** (anion)
3. Opposite charges attract → Strong **electrostatic force** binds them.
4. **Ionic bond** forms
5. Compound formed: **Sodium chloride (NaCl)**

Visual Representation of Ionic Bonding:

- Sodium atom (Na) → Sodium ion (Na$^+$)
- Chlorine atom (Cl) → Chloride ion (Cl$^-$)

[Na$^+$] [Cl$^-$]
[Mg^{2+}] [:F:$^-$]

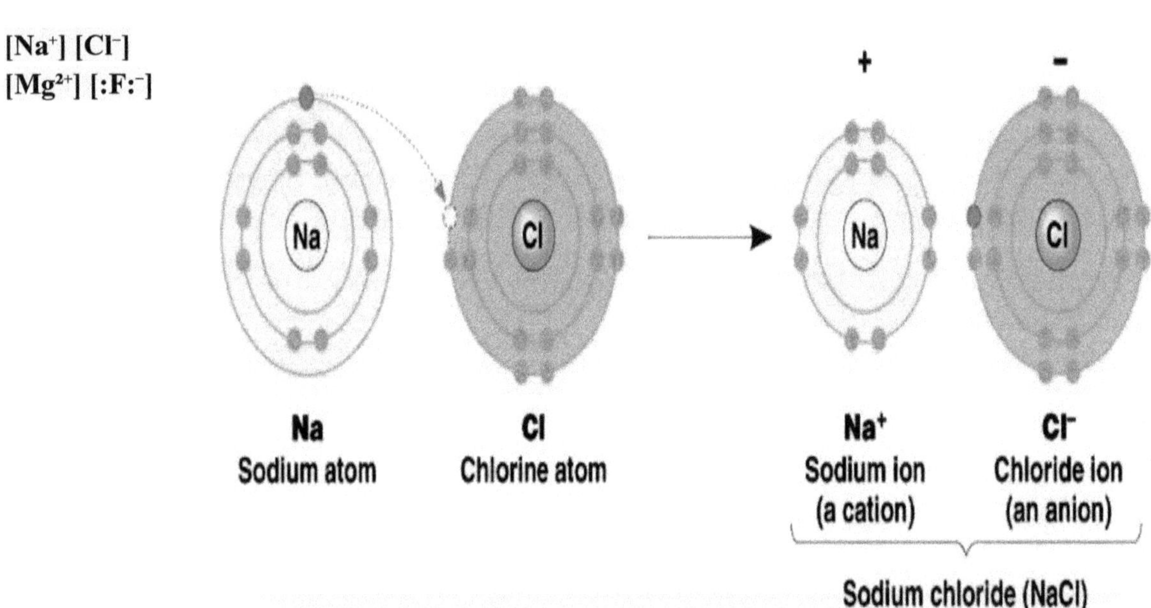

Properties of Ionic Compounds

Property	Description
Physical nature	Solid, hard, brittle due to strong ionic bonds.
Melting & Boiling points	High, due to strong inter-ionic attractions requiring more energy to break.
Solubility	Soluble in water, insoluble in organic solvents like kerosene and petrol.
Electrical conductivity	Conducts in molten and aqueous states, not in solid due to immobile ions.

Basic Concepts in Metallurgy

- **Metallurgy**: Science & tech of metals' properties, production, purification
- **Minerals**: Naturally occurring elements/compounds in Earth's crust
  ↓
- **Ores**: Minerals from which metals can be extracted economically and conveniently
  ↓
- **Gangue Particles**: Impurities in ores (sand, oil, etc.)
  ↓
- **Enrichment of Ore/Concentration**: Process of removing gangue particles from ores

Minerals vs. Ores

Minerals	Ores
Elements or compounds occurring naturally in Earth's crust.	Minerals with a high percentage of metal, profitable for extraction.
May or may not contain metals.	Definitely contain metals.
All minerals are not ores.	All ores are minerals.
Examples: **Salt, Clay, Marble**	**Examples**: Bauxite, Hematite, Rock Salt

Metal Extraction Methods by Reactivity

- **K (Potassium)**
- **Na (Sodium)**
- **Ca (Calcium)**
- **Mg (Magnesium)**
- **Al (Aluminium)**
  - ➤ **Electrolysis**
  - → *Highly reactive metals are extracted using electrolysis.*
- **Zn (Zinc)**
- **Fe (Iron)**

- **Pb (Lead)**
  - ➤ **Reduction using carbon**
  - → *Moderately reactive metals are extracted through carbon reduction.*
- **Cu (Copper)**
- **Ag (Silver)**
- **Au (Gold)**
  - ➤ **Found in native state**
  - → *Low reactivity; found free in nature.*

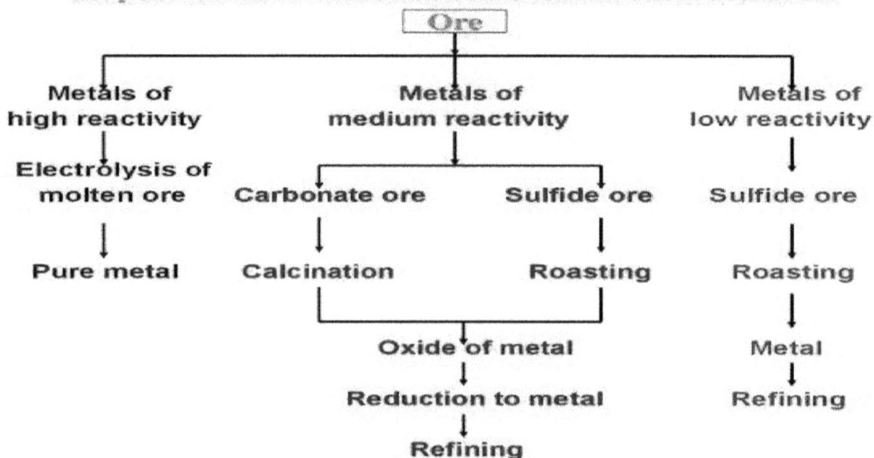

Reactivity	Metals	Process	Key Reactions
Low Reactivity	Mercury (Hg), Copper (Cu)	Reduction by heating	1. $HgS + O_2 \rightarrow HgO + SO_2$ 2. $HgO \rightarrow Hg + O_2$ 3. $Cu_2S + O_2 \rightarrow Cu_2O + SO_2$ $Cu_2O + Cu_2S \rightarrow Cu$
Medium Reactivity	Zinc (Zn), Iron (Fe), Lead (Pb)	Roasting (sulphides), Calcination (carbonates)	1. $ZnS + O_2 \rightarrow ZnO + SO_2$ 2. $ZnCO_3 \rightarrow ZnO + CO_2$ 3. $ZnO + C \rightarrow Zn + CO$
		Reduction using carbon or displacement	$MnO_2 + Al \rightarrow Mn + Al_2O_3$ $Fe_2O_3 + Al \rightarrow Fe + Al_2O_3$ **(Thermite reaction** – highly exothermic)
High Reactivity	Sodium (Na), Magnesium (Mg), Calcium (Ca), Aluminium (Al)	Electrolytic reduction	1. $Na^+ + e^- \rightarrow Na$ 2. $2Cl^- + Cl_2 + 2e^-$ 3. Al_2O_3 (electrolysis) $\rightarrow Al$

Electrolytic Reduction

- **Cathode**: $Na^+ + e^- \rightarrow Na$
- **Anode**: $2Cl^- \rightarrow Cl_2 + 2e^-$

Refining of Metals

- **Electrolytic refining** is widely used for purification.
- Metals like **copper, zinc, tin, nickel, silver, gold** are refined using this method.

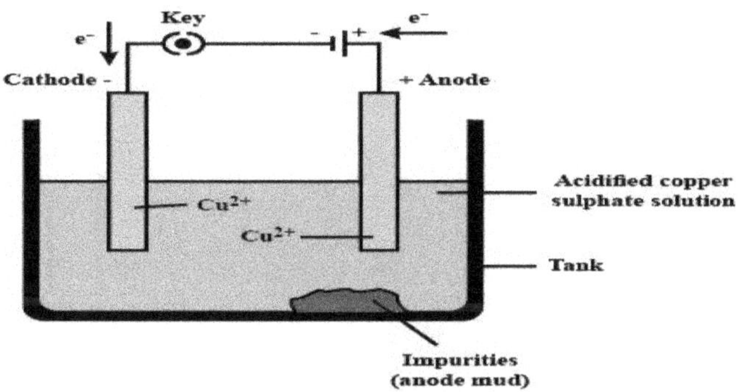

Process:

- **Pure metal is the cathode**
- **Impure metal is the anode**
- **Electrolyte**: Acidified copper sulphate solution
- **Insoluble impurities** form **anode mud**, while soluble ones stay in the solution.

Roasting vs. Calcination

Roasting	Calcination
Heating of a metal ore in the presence of excess air or oxygen.	Heating of a metal ore in the presence of limited air or oxygen.
Requires an excess amount of air or oxygen.	Done with limited air or oxygen.
Mainly done for sulphide ores.	Done for carbonate ores.
Releases toxic gases and substances (e.g., SO_2).	Releases volatile compounds, often less toxic than in roasting.

Corrosion

Metal	Reaction/Result	Prevention Methods	Chemical Reaction
Silver	Turns black when exposed to air due to the formation of silver sulphide.	Painting, oiling, greasing, galvanizing, chrome plating, anodizing, alloying	$4Ag + 2H_2S + O_2 \rightarrow 2Ag_2S + 2H_2O$

Copper	Gains a green coat (copper carbonate) when reacting with moist carbon dioxide.	Galvanization (coating with zinc), alloying (e.g., stainless steel)	$Cu + H_2O + O_2 + CO_2 \rightarrow$ $CuCO_3 \cdot Cu(OH)_2$ (green)
Iron	Forms a brown flaky substance (rust) when exposed to moist air.	Galvanization, alloying, painting, oiling, greasing	$Fe + O_2 + H_2O \rightarrow$ $Fe_2O_3 \cdot xH_2O$ (rust)

Alloying

- An **alloy** is a mixture of metals or a metal with a non-metal, altering properties like conductivity and melting point.

Examples:

- **Brass** (Copper + Zinc) and **Bronze** (Copper + Tin) are poor conductors, unlike Copper, which powers electrical circuits.
- **Solder** (Lead + Tin) melts easily, making it perfect for welding electrical wires.
- **Pure gold** is soft, so it is alloyed with silver or copper to make jewelry, typically in 22-carat form in India.
- The **Iron Pillar** near **Qutub Minar in Delhi**, over **1600 years old**, resists rust due to ancient

  Indian metallurgy techniques.

ACID BASES AND SALTS

Acid vs Base

Acid	Base
Usually sour in taste.	Bitter in taste and soapy to touch.
Turns blue litmus paper red.	Turns red litmus paper blue.
Gives hydrogen ions in solution.	Gives hydroxyl ions in solution.
pH < 7	pH > 7
e.g. **Hydrochloric Acid (HCl), Acetic Acid (CH_3COOH)**	**e.g.** *Sodium Hydroxide (NaOH), Calcium Hydroxide ($Ca(OH)_2$)*

Natural Acids from Sources

Natural Source	Acid	Natural Source	Acid
Vinegar	Acetic acid	Sour milk (Curd)	Lactic acid
Orange	Citric acid	Lemon	Citric acid
Tamarind	Tartaric acid	Ant sting	Methanoic acid
Tomato	Oxalic acid	Nettle sting	Methanoic acid

Indicators

A chemical compound that changes its colour in presence of an acid or a base.

Types:

01 Natural (found in nature)

Indicator	Neutral Solution	Reaction with Acid	Reaction with Base
Litmus	Pale purple (Mauve)	Red	Blue
Hydrangea flowers	Blue	Blue	Pink
Turmeric	Yellow	Yellow	Red

Litmus solution is a purple dye from lichen, used as an indicator.

02 Synthetic (from chemical processes)

Indicator	Reaction with Acid	Reaction with Base
Phenolphthalein	Colourless	Pink
Methyl Orange	Red	Yellow

03 Olfactory Indicators

Substances whose **odour changes** in acidic or basic medium.
Examples: Vanilla, Onion, Clove oil

- In **base**: No smell
- In **acid**: Smell remains

Chemical Properties of Acids

Acid with	Reaction	Example	Key Observations
Metal	Metal + Dilute Acid $\rightarrow$ Salt + Hydrogen Gas	$Zn + 2HCl \rightarrow ZnCl_2 + H_2$	Hydrogen gas evolved; soap bubble test ignites with pop near a burning candle.
Metal Carbonate	Metal Carbonate + Acid $\rightarrow$ Salt + CO_2 + Water	$Na_2CO_3 + 2HCl \rightarrow 2NaCl + CO_2 + H_2O$	CO_2 turns lime water milky.
Metal Hydrogencarbonate	Metal Hydrogen carbonate + Acid $\rightarrow$ Salt + CO_2 + Water	$NaHCO_3 + HCl \rightarrow NaCl + CO_2 + H_2O$	CO_2 turns lime water milky.
Metallic Oxide **(basic)**	Metallic Oxide + Acid $\rightarrow$ Salt + Water *(Neutralization reaction)*	$CuO + HCl \rightarrow CuCl_2 + H_2O$	Blue-green solution indicating $CuCl_2$ formation.

Additional Equation:

$Ca(OH)_2$ (aq) + CO_2 (g) $\rightarrow$ $CaCO_3$ (s) + H_2O (l)
With excess CO_2:
$CaCO_3$ (s) + H_2O (l) + CO_2 (g) $\rightarrow$ $Ca(HCO_3)_2$ (aq)

CHEMICAL PROPERTIES OF BASES:

Reaction Type	Reaction	Example	Key Observations
Base with Metal	Metal + Base $\rightarrow$ Salt + Hydrogen Gas	$Zn + 2NaOH \rightarrow Na_2ZnO_2 + H_2$	Hydrogen gas evolved; indicates a reaction with the base.
Base with Non-Metal Oxide	Non-Metallic Oxide + Base $\rightarrow$ Salt + Water	$CO_2 + Ca(OH)_2 \rightarrow CaCO_3 + H_2O$	Neutralization reaction: forms salt and water, indicating acidic nature of oxide.

Neutralization Reaction:

When an acid and a base react to form water and a salt and involves the combination of H^+ ions and OH^- ions to generate water.

Equation:

Base + Acid $\rightarrow$ Salt + Water
$NaOH + HCl \rightarrow NaCl + H_2O$

- **Phenolphthalein Test:**
    - NaOH solution $\rightarrow$ **pink**
    - NaOH + HCl $\rightarrow$ **colorless**

Both acids and bases are good conductors of electricity.

Dilution

Dilution occurs when an acid or base is mixed with water, reducing the concentration of H_3O^+ or OH^- ions per unit volume, making the acid or base less concentrated.

- **Diluted acid:** Small amount of acid (solute) dissolved in a large amount of water (solvent)
- **Concentrated acid:** Large amount of acid dissolved in a small amount of water

Caution: Acid is **slowly added to water**, never the reverse. Adding water to acid releases **huge heat**, causing explosions or acid burns.

Strength can be estimated using **universal indicator** which shows different colours depending on H^+ concentration.

PH (Potential of Hydrogen)

pH is a measure of the concentration of hydrogen ions in solution.

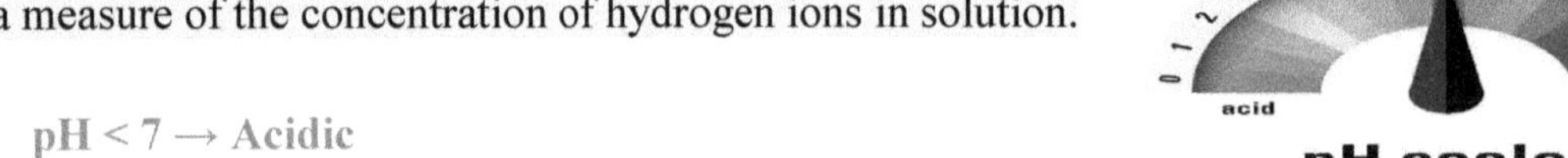

- pH < 7 → Acidic
- pH = 7 → Neutral
- pH > 7 → Basic / Alkaline

Strong acids release more H^+ ions, while **weak acids** release fewer. Same for bases.

Importance of pH in Daily Life:

- **Digestion:**
  The stomach uses hydrochloric acid with pH 1 to 3 to break down food.
- **Soil:**
  Plants grow well in soil with pH 6.3 to 7.3. Too acidic → add lime. Too basic → add gypsum.
- **Tooth Decay:**
  Bacteria make the mouth acidic → tooth decay. Toothpaste (basic) neutralizes it.
- **Blood:**
  Functions best between pH **7.0 to 7.8**.
- **Plants and Animals:**
  Prefer specific pH; most plants thrive near **pH 7**.

- **Bee Stings:**
  Baking soda (base) neutralizes the acid in the sting.
- **Acid Rain:**
  Pollution can lower rain's pH $\rightarrow$ harms aquatic life and the environment.

Salts

Salts are ionic compounds composed of positively charged ions (cations) and negatively charged ions (anions). These ions are held together by ionic bonds.

pH: strong acid + strong base are neutral (pH 7).strong acid + weak base are acidic (pH < 7).strong base + weak acid are basic (pH > 7).

Salts and Their Properties

Salt	pH	Reaction	Origin	Uses
Sodium Chloride ($NaCl$)	Neutral	$HCl + NaOH \rightarrow NaCl + H_2O$ *(common salt)*	Found in seawater and rock salt deposits	Used in food seasoning, raw material for NaOH, baking soda, etc.
Sodium Hydroxide (NaOH)	Basic	$2NaCl + 2H_2O \rightarrow 2NaOH + Cl_2 + H_2$ *(Chlor-alkali process)*	Produced by electrolysis of brine	Used in soap making, paper industry, and as a cleaning agent.
Sodium Hydrogen Carbonate ($NaHCO_3$)	Basic	$NaCl + H_2O + CO_2 + NH_3 \rightarrow NH_4Cl + NaHCO_3$ *(baking soda)*	Produced using sodium chloride, water, CO_2, and ammonia	Used in baking powder, antacids, and soda-acid fire extinguishers.

Salt	pH	Reaction	Origin	Uses
Sodium Carbonate (Na_2CO_3)	Basic	$2NaHCO_3 \rightarrow Na_2CO_3 + CO_2 +$	Obtained by heating sodium	Used in glass, soap, and paper

		H_2O	hydrogen carbonate and recrystallization	industries; removes hardness of water.
Calcium Oxychloride ($CaOCl_2$)	Basic	$Ca(OH)_2 + Cl_2 \rightarrow CaOCl_2 + H_2O$ *(bleaching powder)*	Produced by reacting chlorine with slaked lime	Used in bleaching textiles and paper, disinfecting water, and as an oxidizing agent.
Calcium Sulphate Hemihydrate ($CaSO_4 \cdot \frac{1}{2}H_2O$)	Neutral	$CaSO_4 \cdot 2H_2O \rightarrow CaSO_4 \cdot \frac{1}{2}H_2O + 1\frac{1}{2}H_2O$ *(Plaster of Paris)*	Found as gypsum in natural deposits	Used in making casts (fracture support), toys, decorative items, and for smoothing surfaces.
Sodium Carbonate Decahydrate ($Na_2CO_3 \cdot 10H_2O$)	Basic	$Na_2CO_3 + 10H_2O \rightarrow Na_2CO_3 \cdot 10H_2O$ *(washing soda)*	Produced by recrystallization of sodium carbonate	Used as washing soda, in glass, soap, and paper industries; removes permanent hardness of water.
Copper(II) Sulphate ($CuSO_4 \cdot 5H_2O$)	Acidic	$CuSO_4 \cdot 5H_2O$ (blue) $\rightarrow CuSO_4$ (white) $+ 5H_2O$	Blue crystals found as hydrated copper(II) sulphate	Used in electroplating, as a fungicide, and in chemistry labs to test for water presence.

•**Copper sulphate, contain water molecules in their crystal structure, known as water of crystallisation.**

•**When copper sulphate crystals are heated, they lose their water of crystallisation and turn from blue to white.**

•**Rehydration: Adding water back to the white, anhydrous copper sulphate restores its blue color.**

•**Chemical Formula: The hydrated form of copper sulphate is represented as $CuSO_4 \cdot 5H_2O$, indicating it has five water molecules per chemical unit.**

•At anode: Cl_2 (uses Water treatment, PVC, disinfectants)

•At cathode: H_2 gas (uses Fuels, margarine.)

•Near cathode: NaOH solution formed

•Cl_2 + NaOH → Bleach: household bleaches, bleaching fabrics

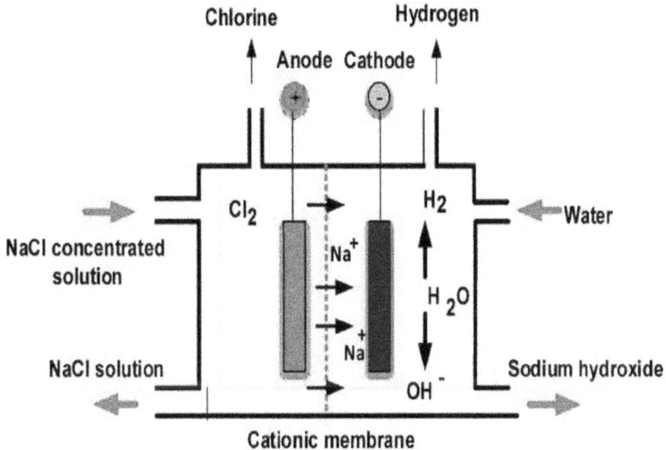

Biology

Faizan bhat

LIFE PROCESSES:

LIFE PROCESS

The basic and essential functions / process performed by living organisms to maintain their life

Nutrition :

The process of obtaining & utilisation of food

Respiration

The process of breaking down of food to obtain energy

Transportation:

The process of transfer of substances from one part of the body to other parts

Excretion:

The process of removal of waste materials produced in the cells of the body

01 NUTRITION

- **AUTOTROPHIC NUTRITION** The organism makes its own food from simple inorganic materials
    - o Example: Green Plants, Autotrophic Bacteria

- **HETEROTROPHIC NUTRITION** Organism cannot make (or synthesize) its own food from simple inorganic materials.
  - o **Holozoic** Organisms consume and internally digest complex organic food e.g. Human beings, Dog, Cat, Amoeba
  - o **Saprophytic** Organisms feed on dead and decaying organic matter e.g. Fungi (bread moulds, mushroom)
  - o **Parasitic** Organisms derive nutrition from another living organism (host), often causing harm to the host e.g. lice, leech, tapeworm, Cuscuta (amer-bel)

PHOTOSYNTHESIS

The process by which plants make their own food from carbon dioxide and water by using sunlight energy in the presence of chlorophyll is called photosynthesis

- **Conditions necessary for photosynthesis** A) Sunlight B) Chlorophyll C) Carbon dioxide D) Water

$$6CO_2 + 12H_2O \rightarrow Chlorophyll \rightarrow Sunlight \rightarrow C_6H_{12}O_6 + 6H_2O + 6O_2$$

1. Absorption of light energy by chlorophyll.
2. Conversion of light energy to chemical energy and splitting of water molecules into hydrogen and oxygen.
3. Reduction of carbon dioxide to carbohydrates.

- **Site of photosynthesis: Chloroplasts** Chlorophyll is present in the green-coloured organelles called "chloroplasts" inside the plant cells. The leaves are green because they contain chloroplasts.

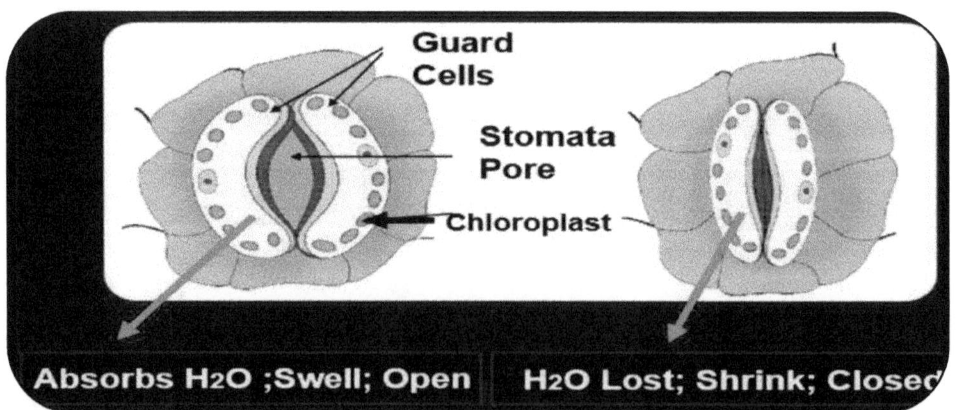

- **CO₂ enters through Stomata** Stomata are tiny pores present on the surface of the leaves

- **WATER - TAKEN UP BY ROOTS FROM SOIL** Nitrogen, phosphorus, magnesium, and iron are taken up in the form of nitrates and nitrites
- **In plants, food (glucose) is stored in the form of starch**
- **In animals, it is stored in the form of glycogen**

Nutrition in AMOEBA

(Unicellular Organism)

1. Amoeba takes in food using temporary finger-like extensions of the cell surface called Pseudopodia
2. Food vacuoles: complex substances → simpler substances
3. Absorption of digested food in cytoplasm by diffusion
4. Undigested food: moves to cell surface and thrown out

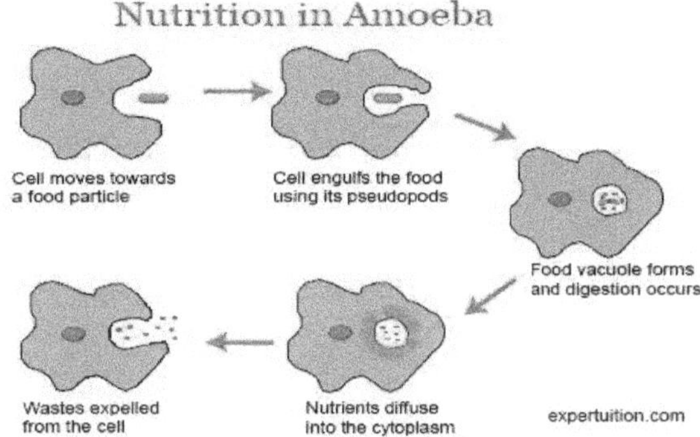

Nutrition in Paramecium

(Unicellular Organism)

1. The cell has a definite shape (like Slipper)
2. Food is moved to a specific spot by the movement of cilia (hair like structure)

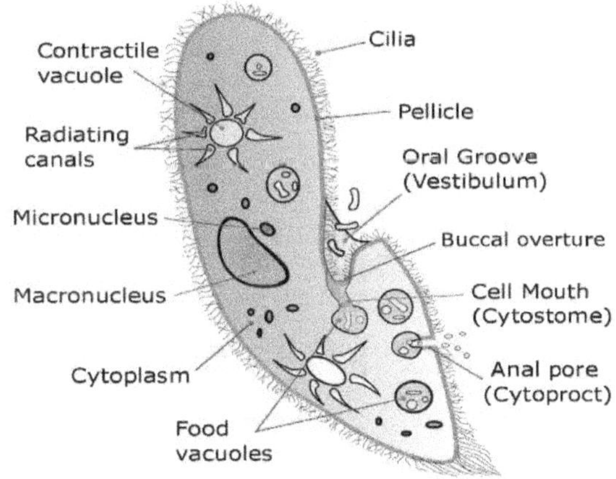

Alimentary Canal → Long tube from Mouth to Anus

- **Teeth:** Crushing/Cut Food in small pieces
- **Liver:** secretes bile juice which is stored in gallbladder. (a) makes acidic food coming from stomach alkaline (b) emulsification of fats – breaks down fats into smaller globules
- **Pancreas:** secretes pancreatic juice
  - trypsin → digests proteins
  - lipase → breaking down of emulsified fats
- **Small Intestine:** coiled; Longest part of alimentary canal
  - site of complete digestion of carbohydrates, proteins and fats.
  - Receives secretion from Liver & Pancreas
- **lots of finger like projections → villi**
  - Villi → supplied with blood vessels
  - Hence, digested food is absorbed and taken to all the cells of body.
- **Salivary Glands:** Secrete Saliva
  - Saliva contains Enzyme → Salivary Amylase
  - Which breakdown Starch (complex Carbohydrates) to simple sugar
- **Oesophagus:** food pipe
  - Peristaltic movement
  - Contraction & Expansion of wall of food pipe
  - Pushes food into stomach
- **Gastric glands**
  - **Hydrochloric acid**
    - Creates Acidic medium for enzyme pepsin
  - **Pepsin**
    - Protein digesting enzyme
  - **Mucus**
    - Protects inner lining of stomach from acid

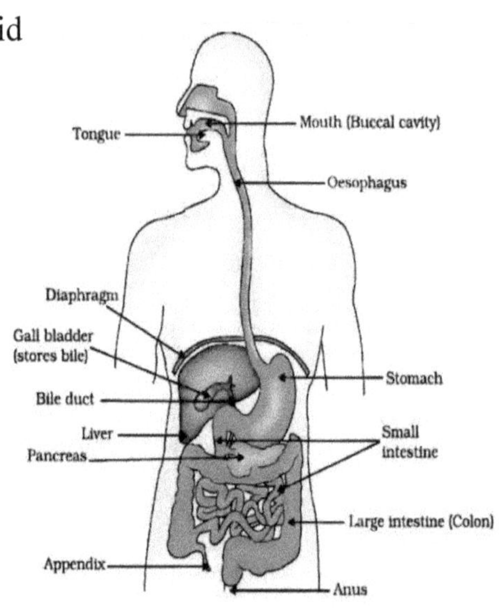

- **Large intestine:**
  - Unabsorbed food → sent to large Intestine
  - Absorbs more water from this material.
  - Rest of the material is removed via anus.
- **Proteins → amino acids**
- **Carbohydrates → glucose**
- **Fats → fatty acid + glycerol**
- exit of waste material via anus is regulated by
- anus sphincter

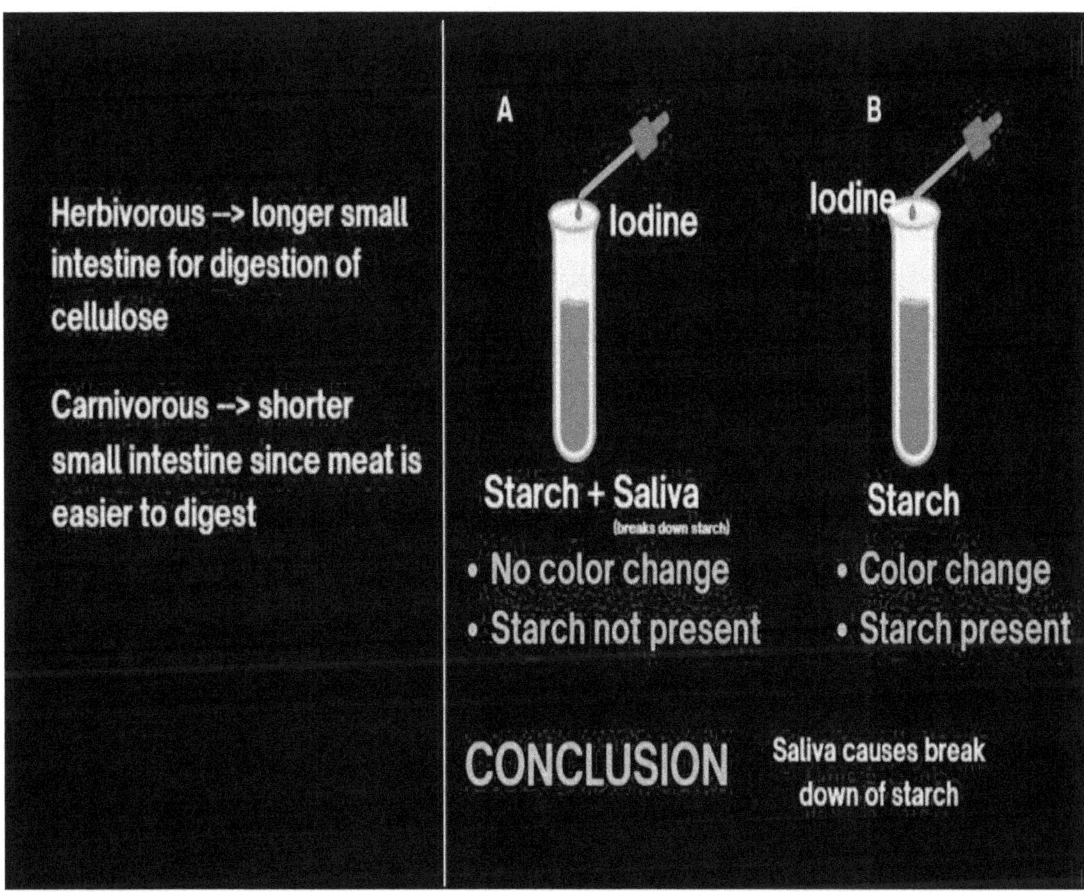

02 RESPIRATION

The process of releasing energy from food is called respiration

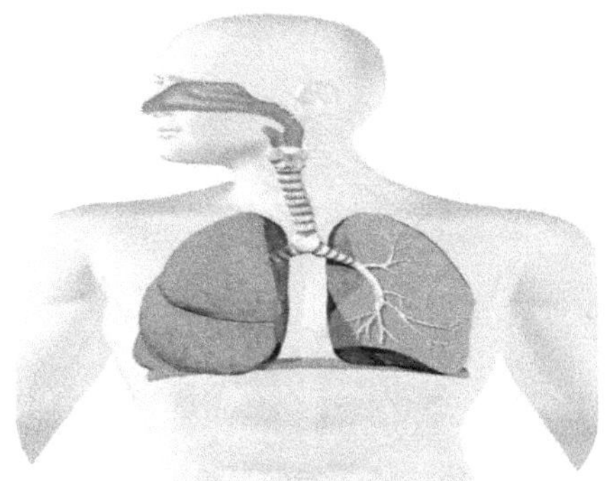

Breathing	Respiration
Physical process	Chemical process
Process of Inhaling & Exhaling the air	Process of breaking down of food to produce energy
No energy released instead energy is required	Energy is released in form of ATP
Happens in lungs	Happens in cells

Glucose (6-carbon molecule) leading to Pyruvate (3-carbon molecule) + Energy

Anaerobic Respiration

- **Absence of Oxygen (in yeast)**
  - Alcoholic respiration/Fermentation
  - Ethanol + Carbon dioxide + Energy (2-carbon molecule)
- **Lack of oxygen (in our muscle cells)**
  - Lactic acid respiration/Fermentation
  - Lactic acid + Energy (3-carbon molecule)
- **Presence of oxygen (in mitochondria)**
  - Carbon dioxide + Water + Energy

Aerobic Respiration

- **The buildup of lactic acid in our muscles during sudden activity causes cramps**

- **Absence of Oxygen (in yeast)**
  - Ethanol + Carbon dioxide + Energy (2-carbon molecule)
- **Lack of oxygen (in our muscle cells)**
  - Lactic acid + Energy (3-carbon molecule)
- **Presence of oxygen (in mitochondria)**
  - Carbon dioxide + Water + Energy

Aerobic Respiration	Anaerobic Respiration
Oxygen is required	Oxygen not required
More Energy produced	Less Energy produced
Complete oxidation and breakdown of glucose	Incomplete oxidation and breakdown of glucose
Occurs in cytoplasm & mitochondria	Occurs only in cytoplasm
End products: CO_2 + H_2O	End products: CO_2 + ethanol / Lactic acid

RESPIRATORY SYSTEM IN HUMAN

- **Nostrils**
  Air enters the passage

- **Nasal Passage**
  Have hairs lining passage for filtration of air
  → Passage lined with mucus
  → To trap dirt and dust and filtration of air
- **Pharynx**
  Common passage for food & air
- **Larynx (voice-box)**
  Produces sound, contains vocal cords
- **Trachea**
  Windpipe
- **Rings of Cartilage**
  Prevents air passage from collapsing
- **Bronchus**
  2 bronchus connect trachea to each lung
- **Bronchioles**
  Each bronchi divides in lungs to form large number of smaller tubes called bronchioles
- **Alveoli**
  Air sacs where exchange of O_2 & CO_2

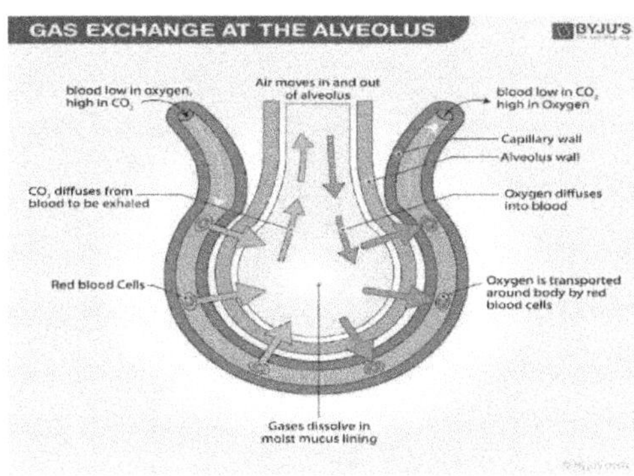

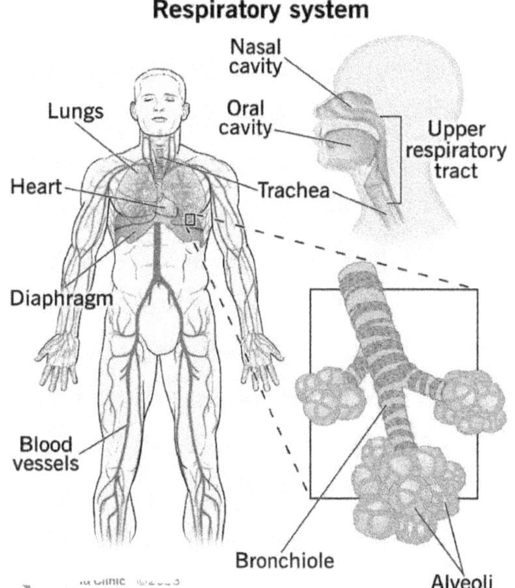

Extra Notes with Diaphragm Image

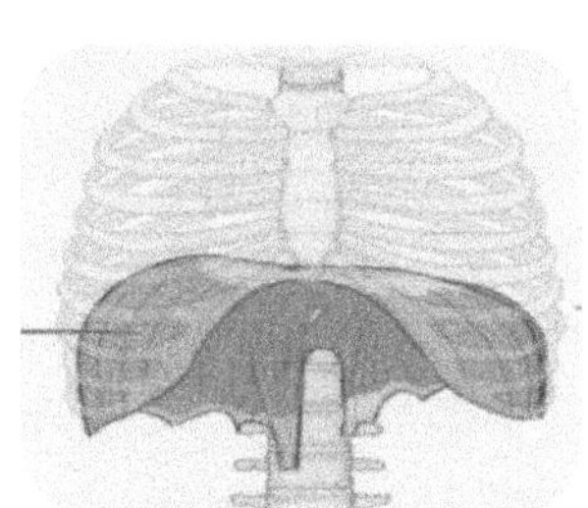

- **The diaphragm is a large, dome-shaped muscle that separates the chest from the abdomen**
- **Residual volume** – *Amount of air always remaining in lungs (to provide sufficient time to absorb O_2 and release CO_2)*

Table: Inhalation / Exhalation

Inhalation / Inspiration	Exhalation / Expiration
Diaphragm contracts	Diaphragm relaxes
Diaphragm moves downward and becomes flat	Diaphragm moves upward and becomes dome-shaped
Chest cavity becomes larger	Chest cavity becomes smaller
Air is sucked into the lungs	Air is pushed out from the lungs

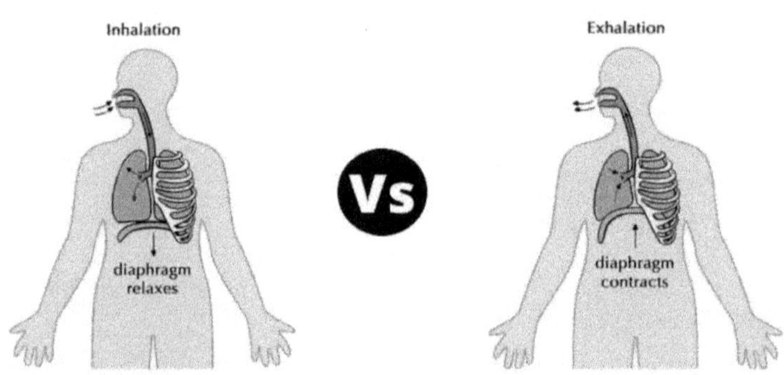

RESPIRATION IN PLANTS

Exchange of gases → Occurs Through Stomata

Day Time:

- Photosynthesis → Oxygen produced
- Respiration → Carbon Dioxide is produced
- This CO_2 is used in Photosynthesis
- **Net Result → O_2 is given out**

Night Time:

- No Photosynthesis
- Respiration → Carbon Dioxide is produced
- **Net Result → CO_2 is given out**

Terrestrial vs Aquatic Organisms

Terrestrial Organisms	Aquatic Organisms
Breathe oxygen in atmosphere	Use dissolved oxygen in water
Rate of breathing is less	Rate of breathing is more

Breathing in Fish

- **Fish take in water through Mouth → force it past the gills → dissolved O_2 is taken by blood**
- *(Mouth open, Gill closed → Vice-Versa)*

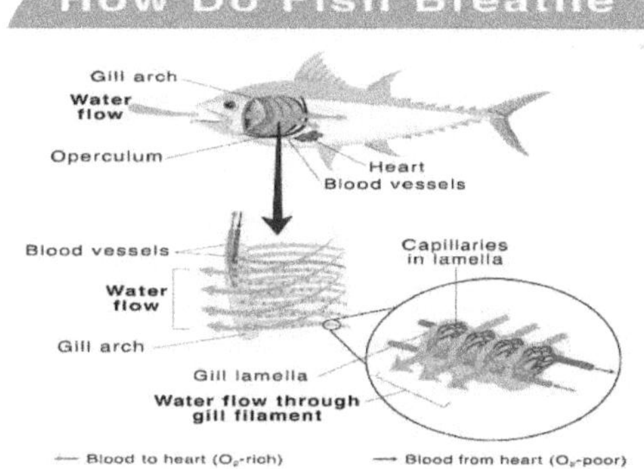

03 TRANSPORTATION

The process of transfer of substances from one part of the body to other parts.

TRANSPORTATION IN HUMAN

- **CIRCULATORY SYSTEM**
- **LYMPHATIC SYSTEM**

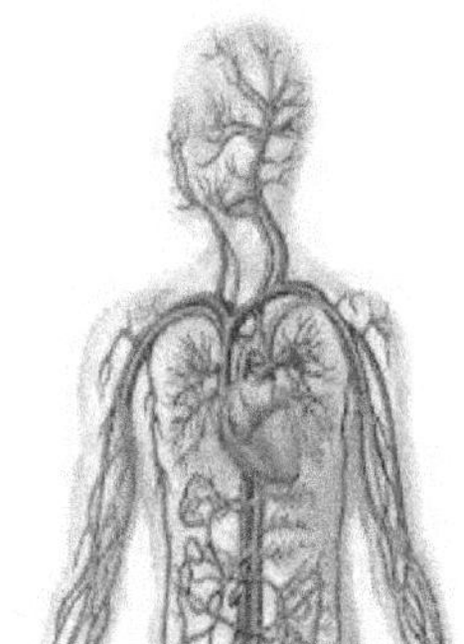

The circulatory system consists of the heart, blood, and blood vessels.

a. HEART

The heart is a muscular organ that is as big as our fist.

- **Ventricles have thicker walls than atria**
  → to withstand high pressure of blood

- **Septum**
  → *Prevents mixing of oxygenated and deoxygenated blood*

Heart Labels and Pathways

- **LUNGS**
  - *Pulmonary vein* (Oxygenated blood)
  - *Pulmonary artery* (Deoxygenated blood)
- **HEART**
  - *Right Atrium*
  - *Right Ventricle*
  - *Left Atrium*
  - *Left Ventricle*
- **Main vein (Vena cava)** – Deoxygenated blood
- **Main artery (Aorta)** – Oxygenated blood
- **Body Organs**

Largest artery – Aorta
Largest vein – Vena cava

Diagram Labels

- **Vena Cava (from upper body & lower body)**
- **Right Atrium**
- **Right Ventricle**
- **Pulmonary Arteries**
- **Pulmonary Veins**
- **Left Atrium**
- **Left Ventricle**
- **Aorta**
- **Septum (dividing wall)**

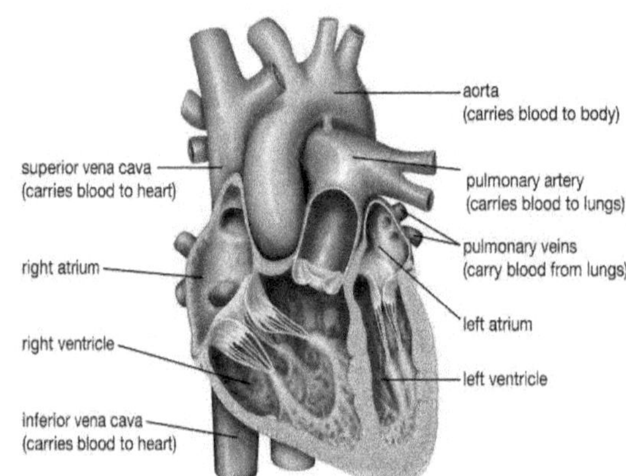

Blood Flow

- **Arteries** – Carry oxygenated blood away from heart
- **Veins** – Carry deoxygenated blood to the heart

- **Pulmonary artery** – *Carries deoxygenated blood*
- **Pulmonary vein** – *Carries oxygenated blood*

b. BLOOD VESSELS

Feature	Arteries	Veins	Capillaries
Direction of Blood Flow	Carries blood away from the heart	Returns blood to the heart	Helps in exchange of substances
Oxygen	Rich in oxygenated blood	Contains deoxygenated blood	Transports both oxygenated & deoxygenated blood
Pressure	High pressure	Low pressure	Moderate pressure
Walls	Thick and elastic walls	Thin and less elastic walls	Very thin (one cell thick)
Valves	Not present	Present (to prevent backflow)	Absent

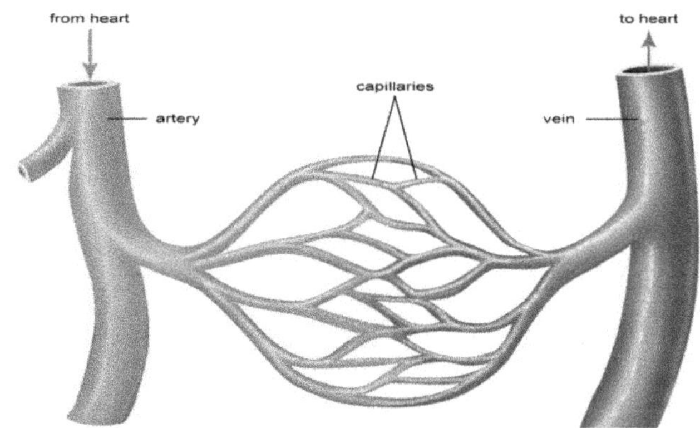

Valves are present in veins to prevent backflow of blood

Exceptions

- **Pulmonary artery** – *Carries deoxygenated blood*
- **Pulmonary vein** – *Carries oxygenated blood*

Double Circulation

Blood flows twice through the heart before completing a full circuit.

Single Circulation

Blood passes only once through the heart in a complete cycle.

Circulation

Animal Group	Heart Chambers	Circulation Type	Body Temperature Regulation
Birds (Aves), Mammals	4	Complete double circulation	Warm blooded
Amphibians, Reptiles	3	Partial double circulation	Cold blooded
Fishes (Pisces)	2	Single circulation	Cold blooded

diagram labels

- Pulmonary artery to lungs
- Lung capillaries
- Pulmonary vein from lungs
- Aorta
- Capillaries in body organs apart from the lungs
- Artery
- Vein
- From body
- To body
- Vena cava

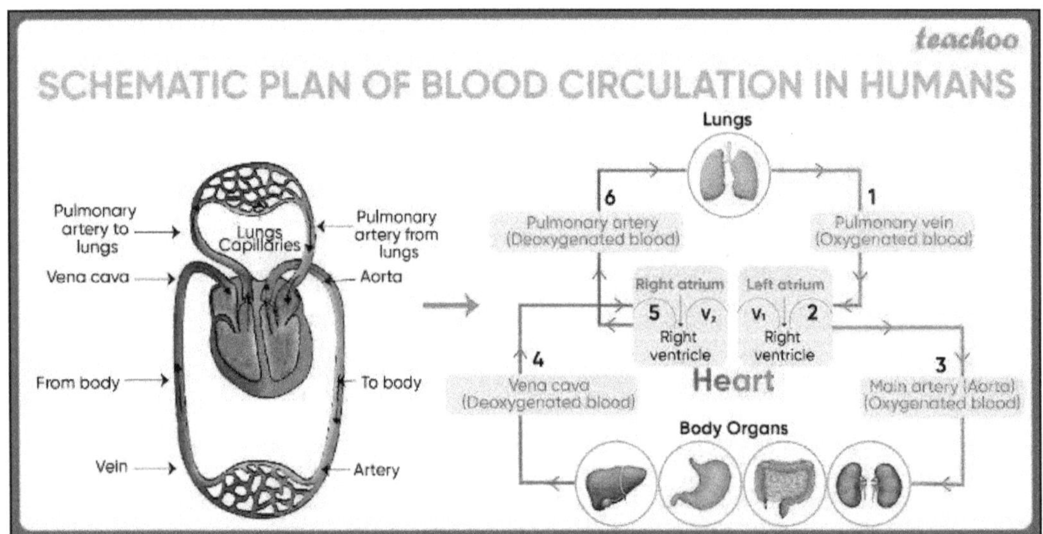

Caption:

Schematic representation of transport and exchange of oxygen and carbon dioxide

c. Blood Components

- **Plasma:** Fluid medium, transports food, carbon dioxide and nitrogenous waste.
- **RBCs:** Contain haemoglobin and transport oxygen
- **WBCs:** Fight infections. Produce antibody to kill pathogens
- **Platelets:** Clotting of blood

Image labels:

- Red blood cells
- Blood vessels
- White blood cells
- Plasma

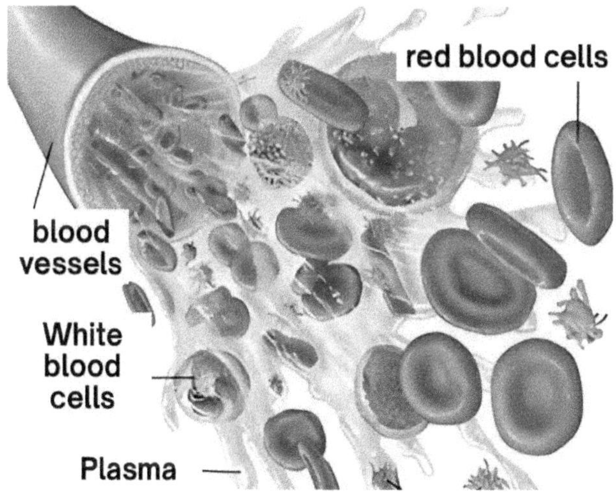

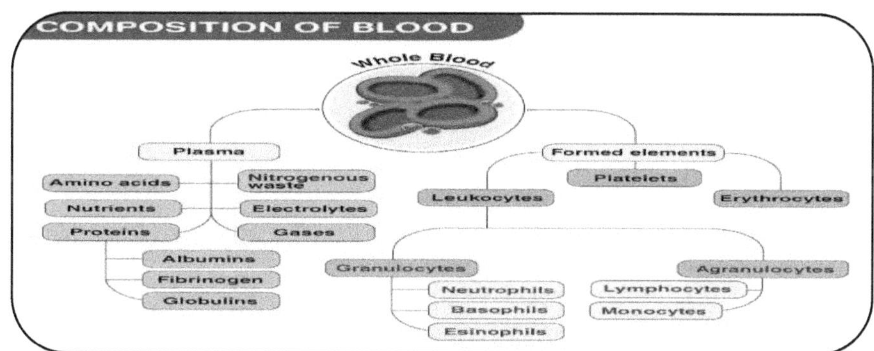

LYMPH or TISSUE FLUID

- Some components of blood leak through pores in walls of capillaries (*plasma, proteins and blood cells - Not RBC*)
- **Lymph is a part of lymphatic system**
- Colourless fluid
- Contains less protein than blood
- Carries digested and absorbed fat from intestine
- Drains excess fluid back into the blood

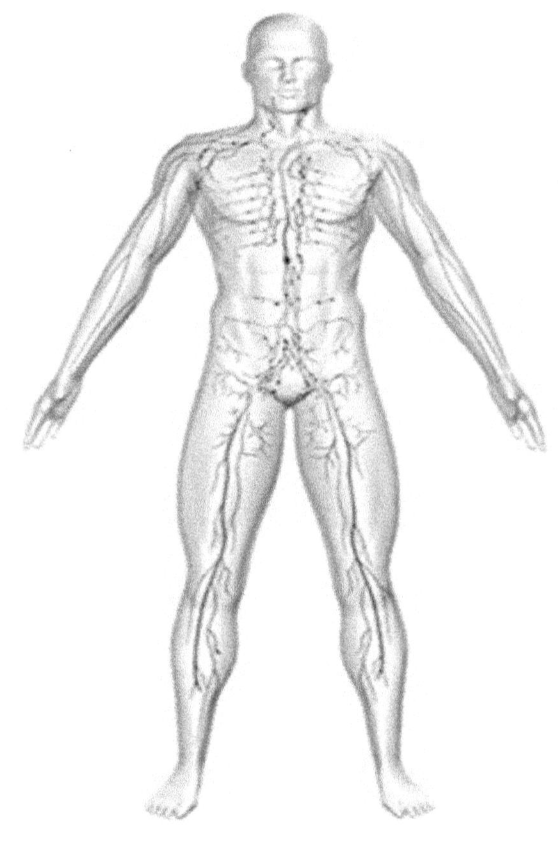

TRANSPORTATION IN PLANTS

Slow transportation system –

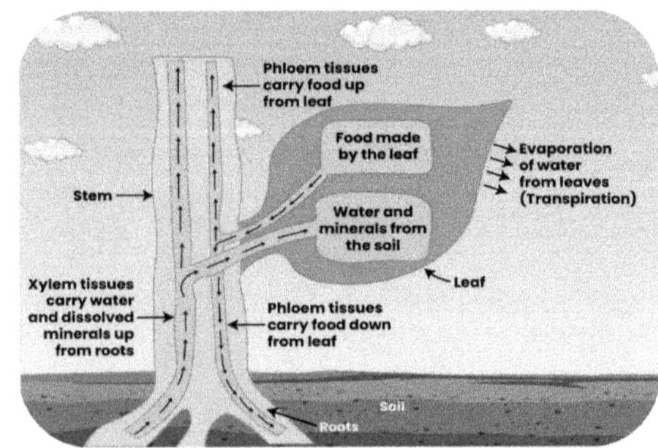

1. Plants do not move
2. Have a large proportion of dead cells in many tissues.
   Hence they have low energy needs and use slow transport systems.
   But, transportation distance can be very large.

Xylem & Phloem are independent conducting tube

Xylem vs Phloem Transport

Feature	Xylem Transport	Phloem Transport
Transports	Water and minerals	Food, amino acids and other substances
Direction of Flow	Unidirectional (upwards from roots to aerial parts)	Bidirectional (both upward and downward)
Process Involved	Physical forces (such as root pressure and transpiration pull)	Active transport (requires energy in the form of ATP)
Main Tissues Involved	Xylem vessels, tracheids	Sieve tubes, companion cells

Transport of water

- **Root pressure** – Roots take up ions from soil which creates difference in the concentration of these ions
- Water from soil moves into the roots
- There is a constant movement of water into root xylem and water is steadily pushed upwards
- **Transpiration** – *The loss of water in the form of vapour from the aerial parts of the plant is called transpiration*

Role of transpiration

1. Absorption and upward movement of water and minerals from roots to leaves
2. Temperature regulation

- Day time – Major force is transpiration pull
- Night time – Root pressure

Transport of food

- **Translocation**

- The transfer of food from leaves to other parts of the plant is called translocation
- Phloem translocates the food made in the leaves
- These substances are especially delivered to the storage organs of roots, fruits and seeds and to growing organs

04.EXCRETION IN HUMAN BEINGS

Removal of harmful metabolic wastes from the body is called excretion.

The excretory system of human beings includes:

- **Kidneys** – Nitrogenous waste such as urea and uric acid are removed from blood through kidneys
- **A pair of ureters** – Connects the kidneys with the urinary bladder
- **Urinary bladder** – Urine is stored in urinary bladder until it is passed out (muscular, under nervous control)
- **Urethra** – Transports urine out of the body

Human Excretory system

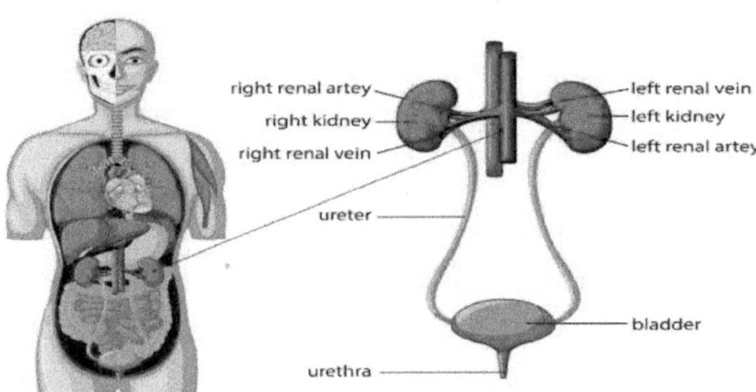

Nephron is the structural and functional unit of kidney.Each kidney has a large number of nephrons.

- **Glomerulus** – Cluster of blood vessels
- **Bowman's Capsule** – Cup-shaped structure in each nephron that surrounds glomerulus and collects the filtrate

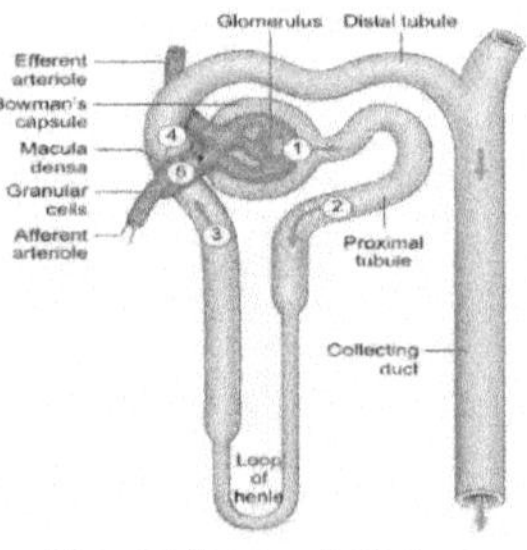

Figure 8.4 Structure of a Nephrons

Processes in the nephron:

- **GLOMERULAR FILTRATION** –
  Nitrogenous wastes, glucose, water, amino acid, excessive salts from the blood are filtered and initial **filtrate** enters into Bowman Capsule of the nephron.
- **SELECTIVE REABSORPTION** –
  Useful substances like glucose, amino acids, salts and a major amount of water from the filtrate are reabsorbed back by capillaries surrounding the nephron.
- **TUBULAR SECRETION** –
  Urea, extra water and salts are secreted into the tubule which open up into the collecting duct & then into the ureter.

Amount of water reabsorbed depends on:

1. Amount of excess water in body
2. Amount of dissolved waste to be excreted

ARTIFICIAL KIDNEY (HEMODIALYSIS)

- In case of kidney failure, an artificial kidney can be used
- An artificial kidney removes nitrogenous waste products from the blood through dialysis
- Artificial kidney --> No reabsorption involved
- **Dialysing fluid** --> same osmotic pressure as blood (without nitrogenous wastes)
- **Used dialysing solution** --> rich in urea and excess salts

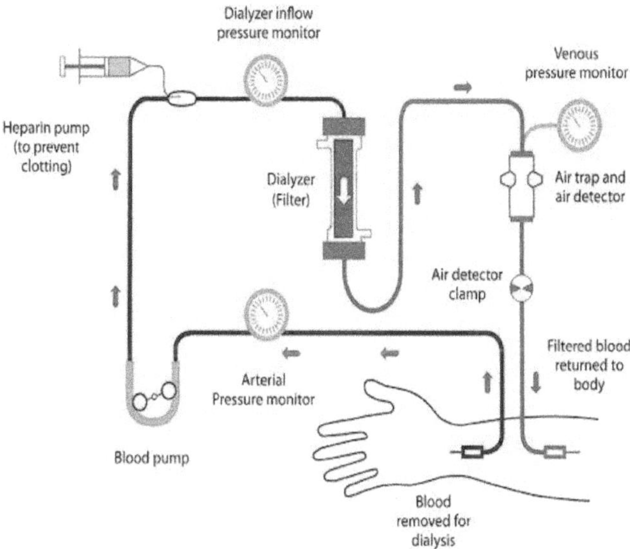

- Oxygen and carbon dioxide --> by diffusion through stomata
- Excess water --> removed by transpiration
- Shedding of old leaves
- Plants also secrete some waste substances into the soil around them

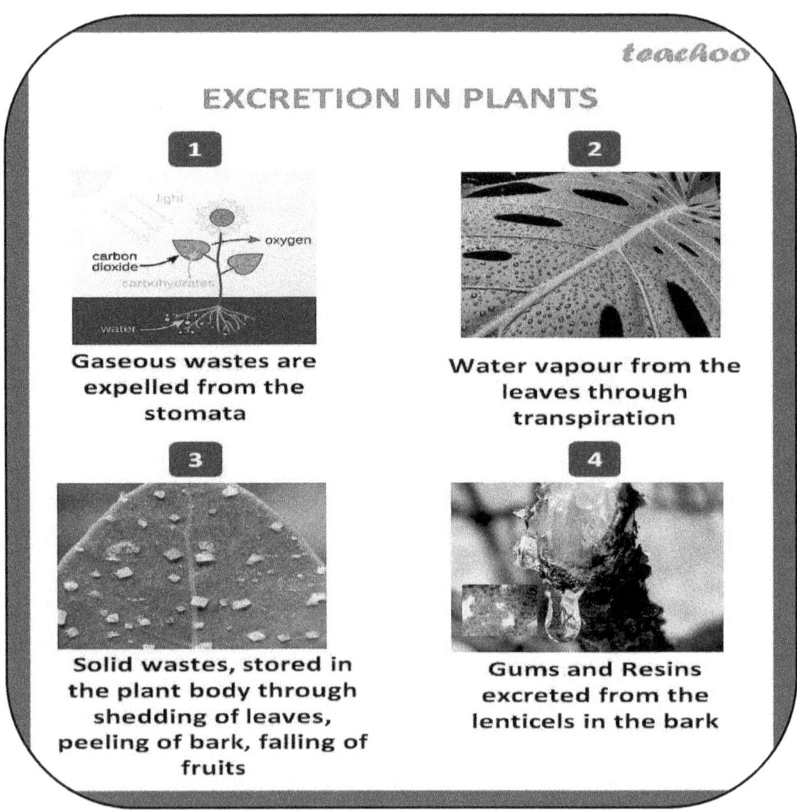

REPRODUCTION

Reproduction is the process by which living organism produce new individuals of the same species

It is Not an essential Life Process

Why important ?

- It ensures the continuity of a particular species on earth
- Population stable

VARIATION

Variations are the differences present between the individuals of the same species

Variation occurs due to – Changes in Genetic material present in Nucleus of cell
Cell --> Nucleus --> Chromosomes --> contain information in form of DNA (Deoxyribo Nucleic Acid)

Replication --> DNA copy

DNA --> Information source for making proteins --> Characteristics
Information changed --> Proteins changed --> Altered body designs

IMPORTANCE OF VARIATION

1. Variation helps organisms to adapt to the changing environment, i.e., provides stability to a species
2. Helps in Evolution of species
3. Variation in DNA results in the varieties of a species and formation of new species

importance of Reproduction

1. Continuity of species (Population Stability)
2. Evolution
3. Variation

ASEXUAL REPRODUCTION

- Single parent is involved
- No Gamete formation
- No Fertilisation
- Offsprings formed are usually genetically similar
- **Fission**
- **Fragmentation**
- **Regeneration**
- **Budding**
- **Vegetative Propagation**
- **Spore Formation**

01.SEXUAL REPRODUCTION

- Two parents are involved
- Gamete formation occurs
- Fertilisation occurs
- Offsprings formed are genetically dissimilar
- **Reproduction in flowering plants**
- **Reproduction in human beings**

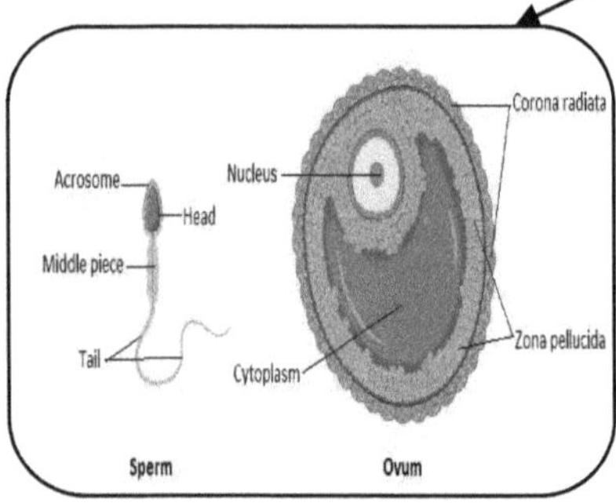

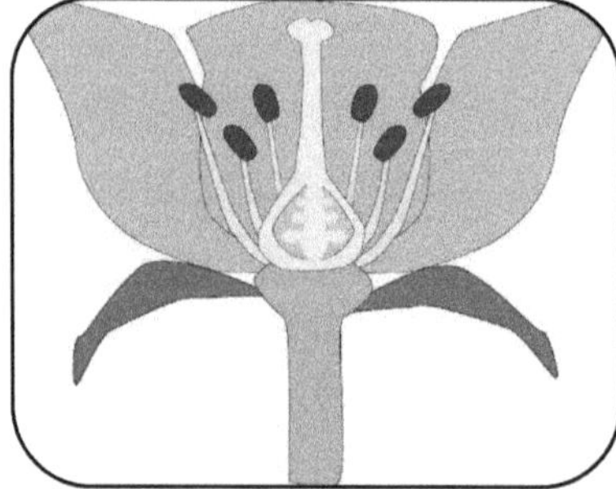

02.ASEXUAL REPRODUCTION

(Unicellular organisms - Cell division)

- **Binary fission in Amoeba**
    - o Occurs in many bacteria and protozoa
    - o Amoeba - unicellular organism
    - o Binary fission in amoeba
    - o Splitting of cells can take place in any plane
    - o Parent cell divides into two daughter cells

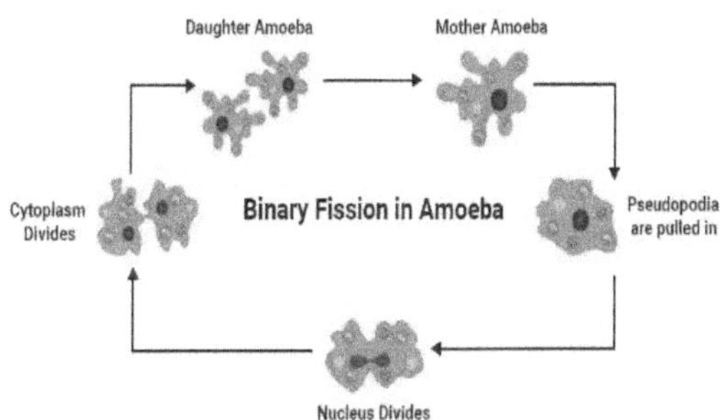

- **Binary fission in Leishmania**
    - o Unicellular organism
    - o Has a whip-like structure at one end of cell
    - o Binary fission occurs in fixed plane (in relation to whip-like structure - Longitudinal fission)
    - o Causes kala-azar

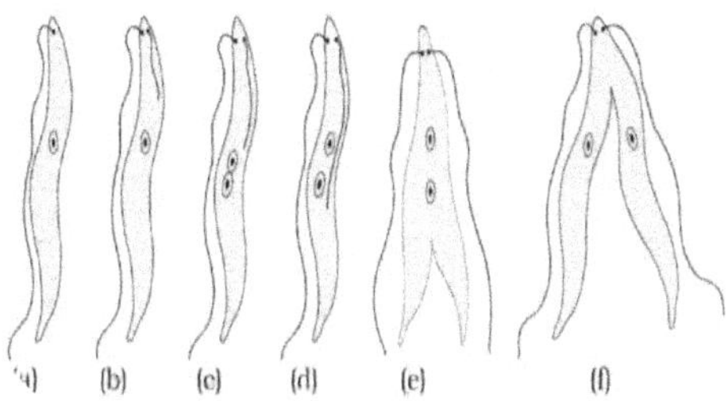

- **Multiple fission in Plasmodium**
    - o Unicellular organism
    - o Divides by multiple fission
    - o Malarial parasite

FRAGMENTATION

- Multicellular organism - spirogyra
- Breaks into smaller pieces upon maturation
- These pieces (fragments) grow into new individuals

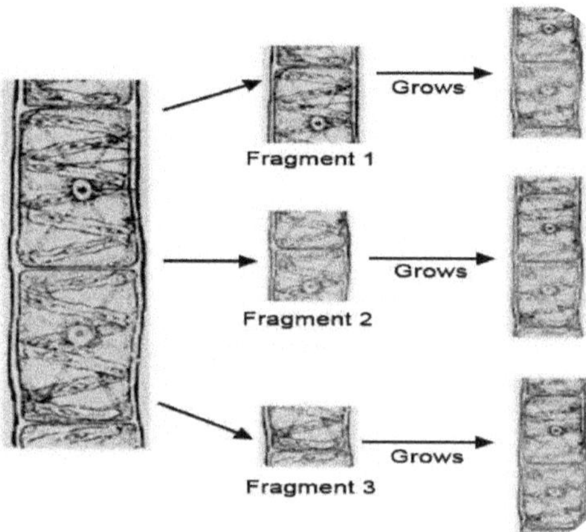

REGENERATION

- If the individual is cut or broken up into many pieces, many of these pieces grow into separate individuals.
- e.g. Planaria and hydra (multicellular organisms)
- **Regeneration in Planaria**
  - o Carried out by specialized cells
- **REGENERATION ≠ REPRODUCTION**

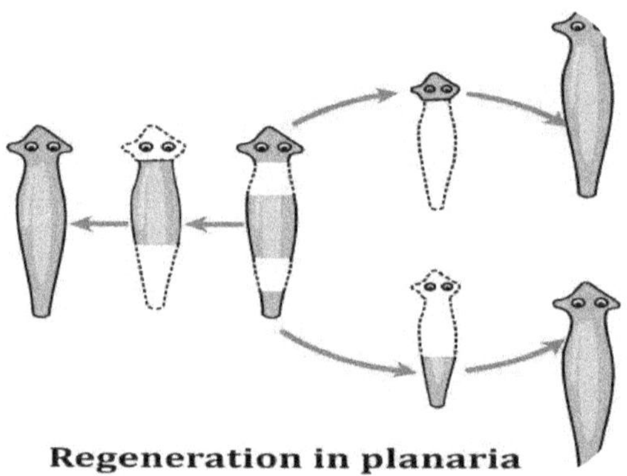
Regeneration in planaria

BUDDING

- e.g. Hydra - Aquatic animal
- **Budding in Hydra**
  - o Hydra - use regenerative cells for reproduction
  - o Repeated cell division at one specific site

- o Outgrowth → bud develops
- o Buds develop into tiny individuals
- o Detach from the parent body on maturation
- o Become new independent individuals

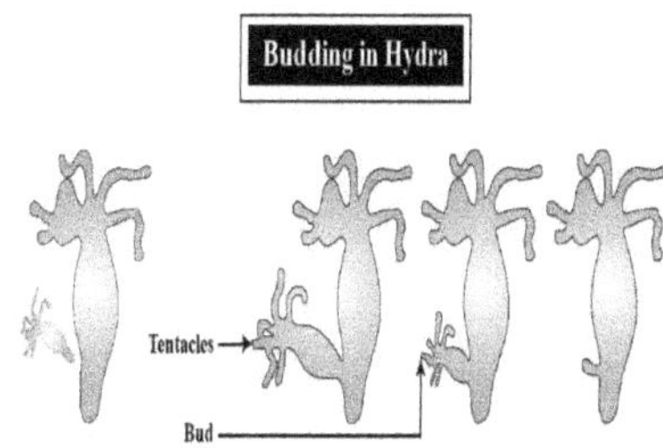

SPORE FORMATION

rhizopus (bread mould) --> multicellular organism (fungus)

- thread like structures - hyphae

- blob on a stick structure - sporangia

- spores develop into new individuals

- covered by thick walls that protects them in unfavourable conditions

- favourable condition - moist surface - spores begin to grow

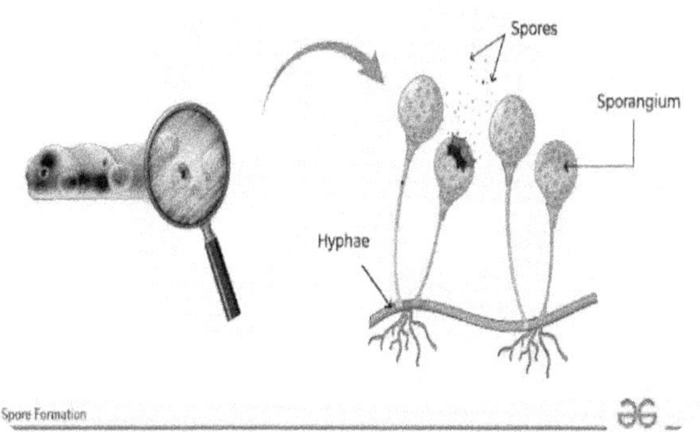

VEGETATIVE PROPAGATION

parts like roots, stems, and leaves develop into new plants

Potato- Underground stem

- Eyes

- Buds

leaf of bryophyllum with buds

Buds produced in the leaf margin of Bryophyllum the soil and develop into new plants

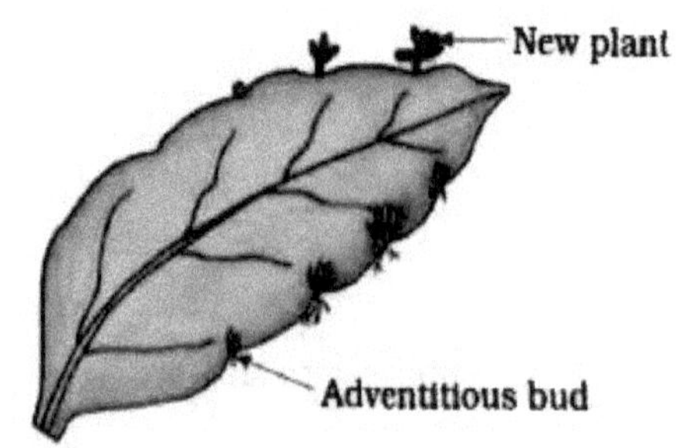

Leaf buds of Bryophyllum

Advantages

- Used in layering or grafting to grow plants like sugarcane, roses, grapes

- propagation of plants that have lost the capacity to grow seeds (banana, orange, rose and jasmine)

- bear fruits and flowers earlier than those produced from seeds

- Plants produced are genetically similar to the parent plant & its characteristics

Layering

Grafting

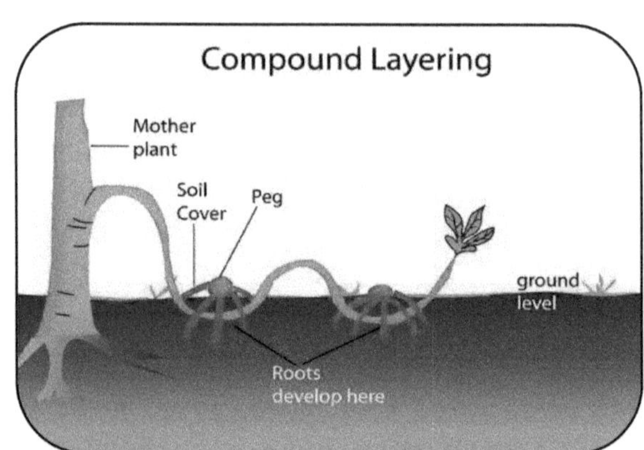

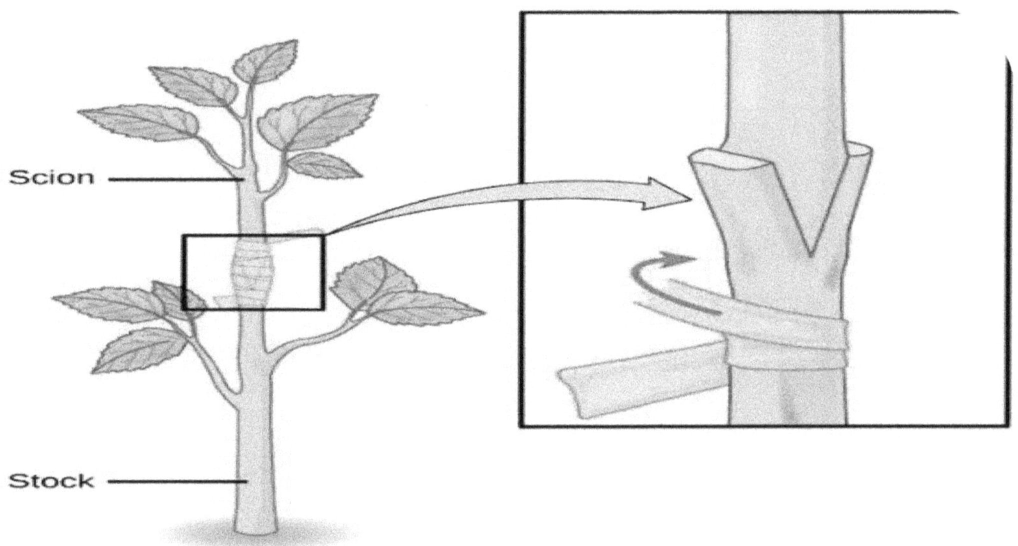

01. CUTTING = A PART OF PLANT TO GROW A NEW PLANT
02. GRAFTING = JOINING A PART OF ONE PLANT TO ANOTHER PLANT
03. LAYERING = BENDING A BRANCH TO TOUCH THE GROUND TO GROW ROOTS

Organism	Cellularity	Mode of reproduction	Disease
Amoeba	Unicellular	Binary fission (any plane)	
Leishmania	Unicellular	Binary fission (fixed plane)	Kala azar
Plasmodium	Unicellular	Multiple fission	Malaria

Spirogyra	Multicellular	Fragmentation
Planaria	Multicellular	Regeneration
Hydra	Multicellular	Budding, Regeneration
Yeast	Multicellular	Budding
Rhizopus	Multicellular	Spore formation

01. SEXUAL REPRODUCTION IN FLOWERING PLANTS (ANGIOSPERMS)

- male reproductive part - stamen (produces pollen grains)

- female reproductive part - pistil

- unisexual flowers - contain either stamen or pistil (papaya or watermelon)

- bisexual flowers - contain both stamens and pistil (hibiscus, mustard)

PISTIL

- Stigma - sticky terminal part

- Style - middle elongated part

- Ovary - swollen bottom part

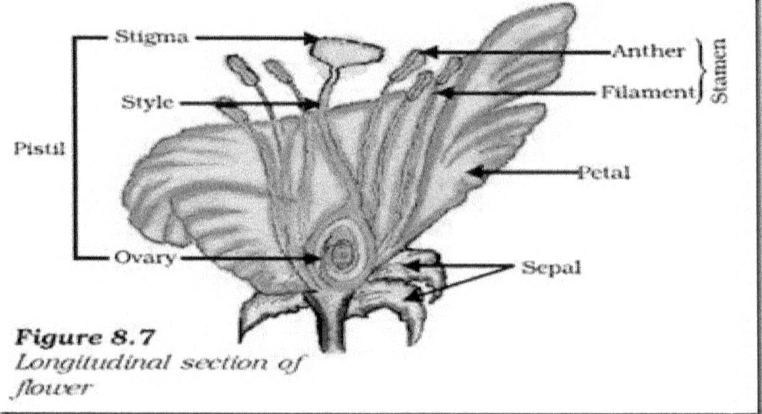

Figure 8.7
Longitudinal section of flower

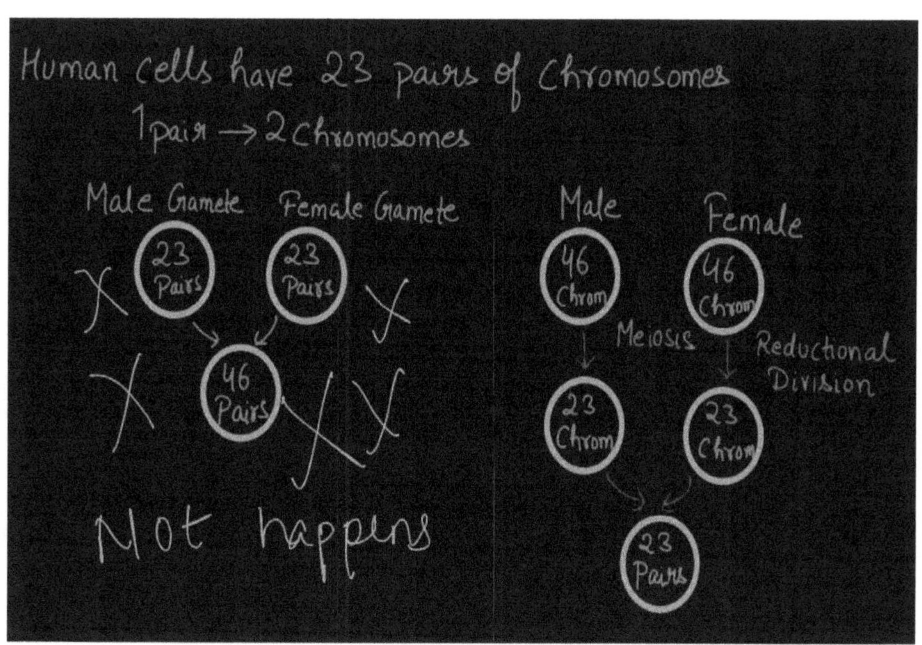

OVARY

- contains ovules

- contains egg cell

Anther contains pollen sac

pollen sacs contains pollen grains

pollen lands on stigma

a tube grows out of the pollen grain

male germ cell + female germ cell

Fertilisation

zygote

multiple division in embryo (within ovule)

OVARY   FRUIT

OVULE   SEED

ZYGOTE   EMBRYO

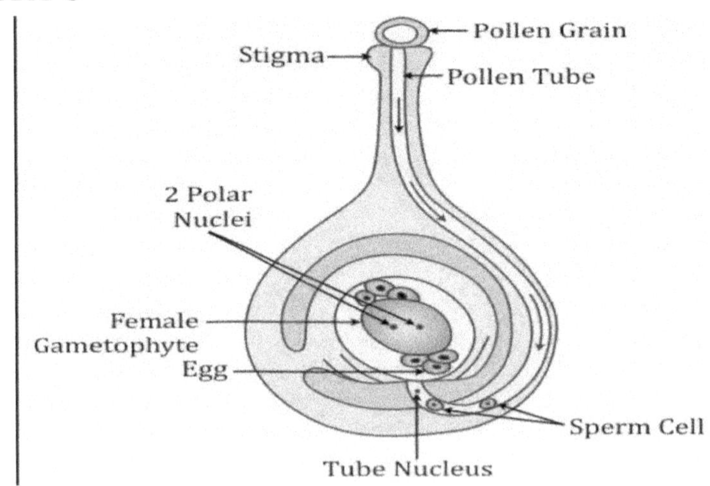

zygote --> embryo

ovule --> seed

- ovary --> fruit

- petals, sepals, stamen, style --> shrivel and fall off

Pollination - transfer of pollen from anther to stigma of a flower

Self pollination

Transfer of pollen in the same flower or another flower in the same plant

Cross pollination

Transfer of pollen from one flower to another

- Agents of pollination

  - wind, water, animals

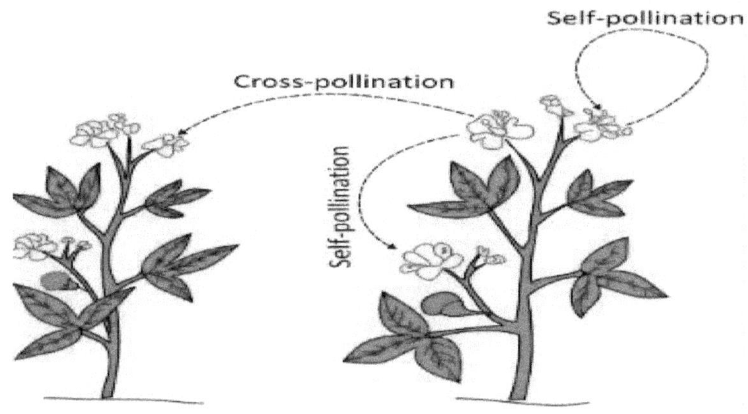

GERMINATION

development of seed into seedlings under appropriate conditions

- Cotyledon (food store)

- Plumule (future shoot)

- Radicle (future root)

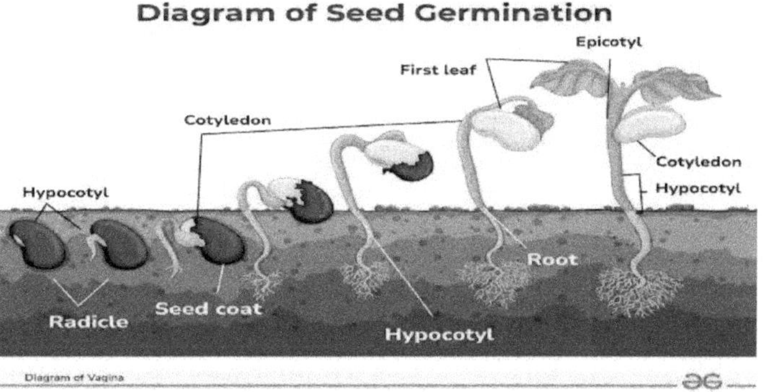

02 SEXUAL REPRODUCTION IN HUMAN BEINGS

Adolescence - the phase of life between childhood and adulthood

 Puberty - The time in life, when a boy or girl becomes sexually mature. It is a process that usually happens between ages 10 and 14 for girls and ages 12 and 16 for boys. It causes physical changes, and affects boys and girls differently. This period during adolescence, general rate of growth decreases.

Common changes in boys and girls

- thick hair growing in new parts of the body (armpits and genital areas)
- darkening of these parts
- thinner hair on legs, arms, and face
- skin becomes oily, develops pimples

Changes in boys

- thick hair growth on face
- voice begins to crack
- penis occasionally begins to become enlarged and erect

Changes in girls

- breast size increases
- darkening of nipples
- menstruation
- All of these changes take place slowly, over a period of months and years.
- They do not happen all at the same time in one person.
- In some, they happen early and quickly, while in others, they can happen slowly.
- male germ cell - sperm
- female germ cell - ovum

A. MALE REPRODUCTIVE SYSTEM

Scrotum

- maintains the lower temperature of the testis (2-2.5°C lower than the normal internal body temperature)
- Produce male sex hormone testosterone
- regulates production of sperms
- changes the body at puberty

Testis Vas deferens

- Carries sperm towards urethra

Urethra

- common passage for both semen (sperm) and urine

Seminal vesicle and Prostate gland

- Add a fluid which makes their transport easier

Penis

- Provides nutrition
- deposits sperm into vagina during insemination
- sperms are tiny bodies that consist of mainly genetic material and a long tail that helps them to move towards female germ cell

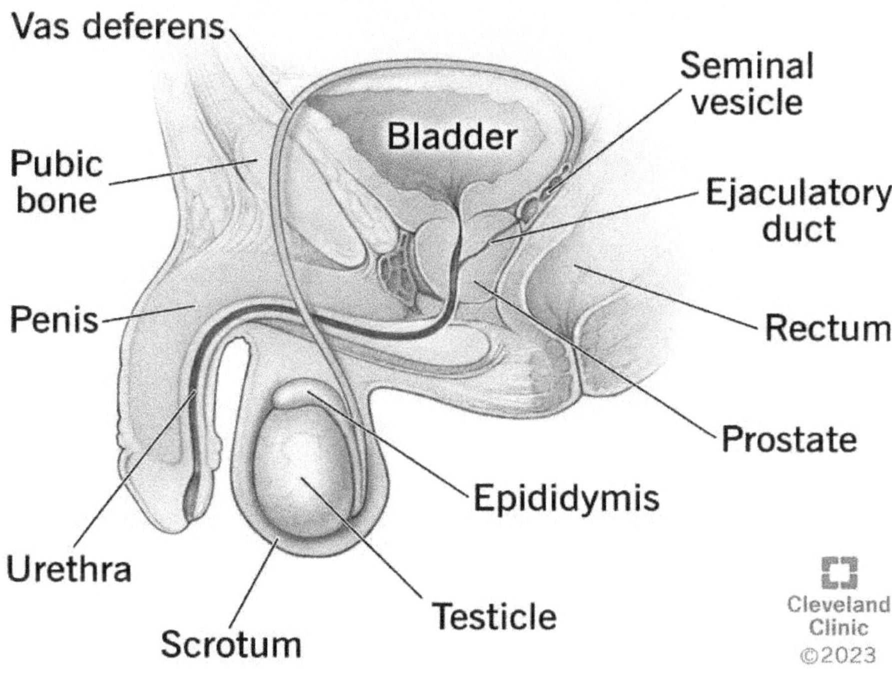

B. FEMALE REPRODUCTIVE SYSTEM

Ovary

- one egg cell development
- The ovary releases one egg every month

FALLOPIAN TUBES (OVIDUCTS)

- carry the ovum from the ovary to the uterus
- if the egg is not fertilised, it lives for about one day

Uterus (WOMB)

- elastic bag-like structure in which the embryo and foetus develop
- involved in menstruation
- cervix
    - Separates the vagina from the uterus
    - dilates during birth to allow the foetus to leave the uterus

Vagina

- provides a passageway for sperm and menstrual functions as the birth canal

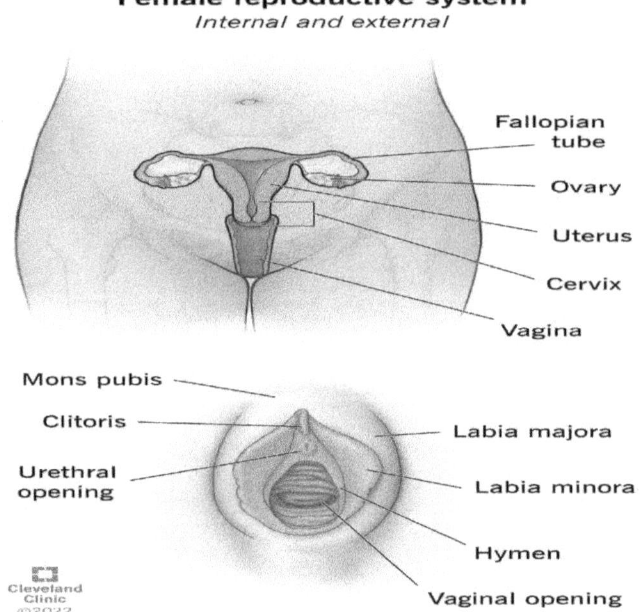

SEXUAL INTERCOURSE

- penis is inserted into the vaginal passage -> travel upwards
- reaches ovary duct -> encounters ovum -> Fertilization

- Fertilized egg (zygote) -> divides to form a ball of cells (embryo)
- implanted in the lining of the uterus
- organs to become foetus
- The uterus prepares itself every month to receive the embryo
- if no fertilisation occurs, and implantation does not take place, the lining slowly breaks and passes out through the vagina as blood and mucus

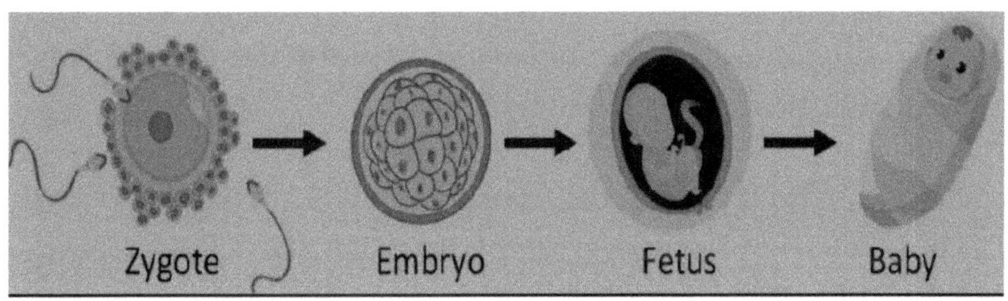

PLACENTA

- disc embedded in the uterine wall
- provides nutrition to embryo from mother's blood
- Villi on placenta (embryo side) provides a large surface area for
  - glucose and oxygen to pass from the mother to the developing embryo
  - wastes to pass from the embryo to the mother through the placenta.
- the ovary releases one egg every month
- the uterus also prepares itself every month to receive a fertilised egg.
- Thus its lining becomes thick and spongy for nourishing the embryo if fertilisation had taken place.
- however, the lining is not needed any longer if fertilisation does not occur

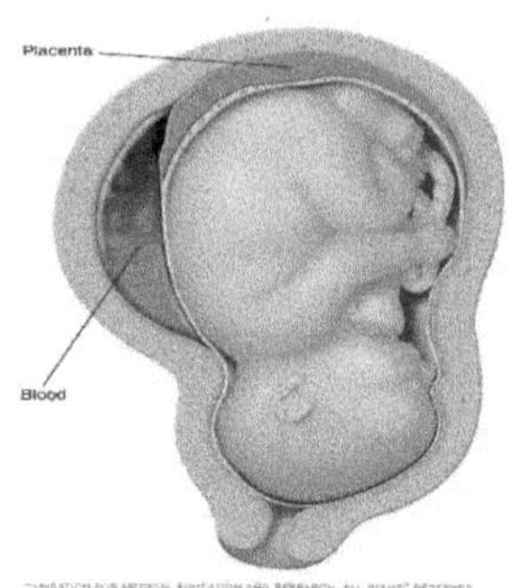

MENSTRUATION The process of shedding the uterine lining leading to vaginal bleeding on a regular monthly basis

GIRL CHILD → MENARCHE → MENOPAUSE → OLD AGE
BEGINNING OF MENSTRUATION STOPPAGE OF MENSTRUATION

Contraceptive Methods= THE METHODS WHICH ARE USED TO PREVENT PRAGNANCY

Physical/Mechanical Barrier

Prevents union of sperm and egg.

Protects from sexually transmitted diseases (STDs) such as gonorrhea, syphilis, HIV-AIDS, and warts.

Example: Condoms. DIAPHAPHRAGM

Hormonal Barrier

Oral contraceptive pills (OCPs) change hormonal balance to prevent egg release in females.

Taken orally.

Oral contraceptives may cause side effects.

EG= ORAL PILLS , IMPLANTS , INJECTIONS

IUCD (Intrauterine Contraceptive Device)

A Copper-T or loop is placed in the uterus to prevent pregnancy.

Can cause irritation of the uterus.

Surgical Barrier

Vasectomy: The vas deferens in males is blocked to prevent sperm transfer.

Tubectomy: The fallopian tubes in females are blocked to prevent eggs from reaching the uterus.

Why is DNA copying an essential part of the process of reproduction?

Answer: DNA (Deoxyribonucleic acid) copying is an essential part of reproduction as it passes genetic information from parents to offspring. It determines the body design of an individual. The reproducing cells produce a copy of their DNA through some chemical reactions and result in two copies of DNA. The copying of DNA always takes place along with the creation of additional cellular structure. This process is then followed by division of a cell to form two cells.

What is the importance of DNA copying in reproduction?

Answer:

DNA (Deoxyribonucleic acid) is the genetic material found in the chromosomes, which are present in the nucleus of a cell. The DNA is the information site for making proteins and each specific type of protein leads to a specific type of body design. Thus, it is the DNA molecule that determines the body design of an individual. Therefore, it can be concluded that it is the DNA that gets transferred from parents to offsprings and makes them look similar.

DNA determines body structure

Why is variation beneficial to the species but not necessarily for the individual?

Answer:

Variations are beneficial to the species than individual because sometimes for a species, the environmental conditions change so drastically that their survival becomes difficult. For example, if the temperature of water increases suddenly, then most of the bacteria living in that water would die. Only few variants that are resistant to heat would be able to survive. However, if these variants were not there, then the entire species of bacteria would have been destroyed. Thus, these variants help in the survival of the species. However, all variations are not necessarily beneficial for the individual organisms.

CONTROL AND COORDINATION

.1 Introduction to Coordination

Term	Definition
Coordination	Working together of various organs of an organism to adjust various activities of life.
Stimuli	Change in the environment that can cause a physical or behavioral change in a living organism.
Response	The reaction of an organism to an internal or external stimulus.

2. Receptors and Effectors

Type	Function
Receptors	Cells or groups of cells in sense organs that detect stimuli and convert them into impulses.
Effectors	Parts of the body that respond to impulses sent by the nervous system (e.g., muscles and glands).
Receptor Type	**Organ/Function**
Photo receptors	Eyes
Phono receptors	Ears
Thermo receptors	Skin
Olfactory receptors	Nose
Gustatory receptors	Tongue

3. Coordination in Animals

System	Sub-Systems	Details
Nervous System	Central Nervous System	Brain (Forebrain, Midbrain, Hindbrain), Spinal cord
	Peripheral Nervous System	Cranial Nerves(12 PAIR) (from brain), Spinal Nerves (PAIR)(from spinal cord)
Endocrine System	Hormones	

Neurons

Part	Function
Dendrites	Acquires information
Cell body	Acquired information travels as an electrical impulse
Axon	Longest fiber; transmits electrical impulse from cell body to dendrite of next neuron
Nerve Ending	Final part of axon, connects to other neurons or effectors
Synapse	Gap between axon of one neuron and dendrite of another; converts electrical signal $\rightarrow$ chemical signal

| **Special Note** | **Neuromuscular Junction (NMJ)**: Synaptic connection between a motor neuron and a muscle |

| **Flow** | Dendrites $\rightarrow$ Cell Body $\rightarrow$ Axon $\rightarrow$ Nerve Ending $\rightarrow$ Synapse |

Types of Neurons

Type	Function
Sensory Neurons	Transmit impulses from sense organs to brain
Motor Neurons	Transmit impulses from brain/spinal cord to body
Relay Neurons	Allow sensory and motor neurons to communicate

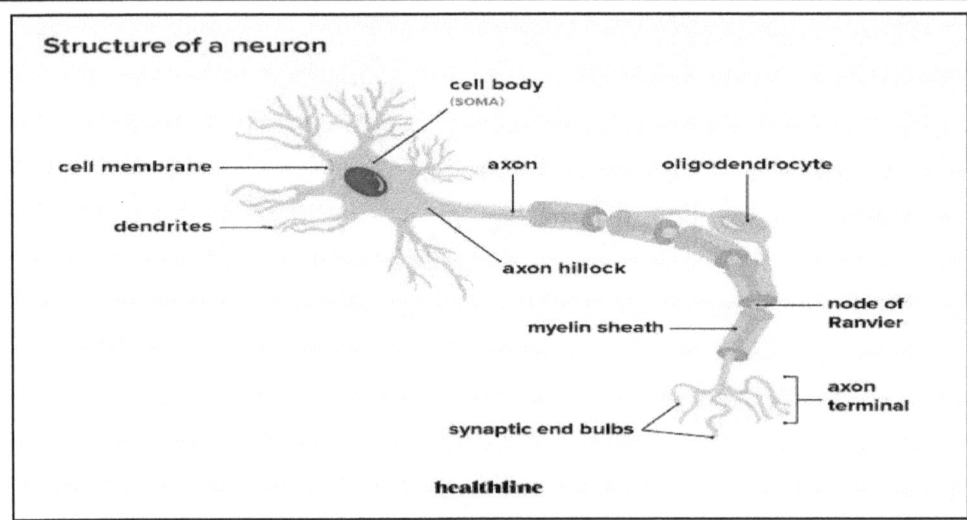

Comparison: Voluntary, Involuntary, Reflex Actions

Aspect	Voluntary Actions	Involuntary Actions	Reflex Actions
Definition	Actions under conscious control	Actions without conscious control	Sudden, automatic responses
Control	Involves the brain's thinking and decision	Controlled by brain stem or spinal cord	Controlled by the spinal cord and reflex arc
Examples	Walking, writing, speaking	Heartbeat, digestion, breathing	Pulling hand away from hot object

Reflex Action

- **Definition**: Spontaneous automatic and involuntary response.
- **Monitored through**: The **spinal cord**.

- The pathway taken by nerve impulses in a reflex action is called a **reflex arc**.

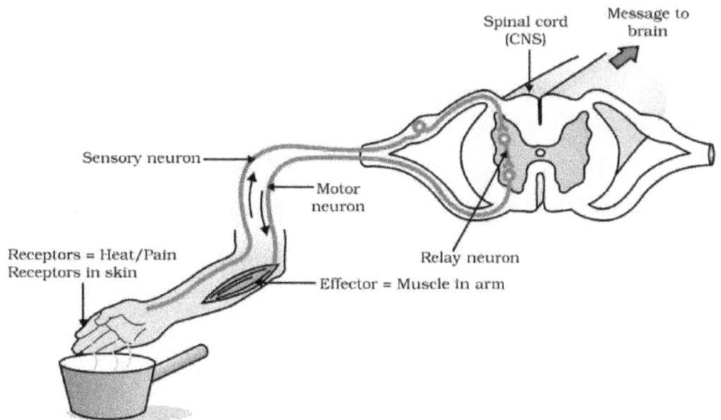

Reflex Arc Pathway:

Stimulus → Receptors → Spinal cord → Effector → Response (Motor neuron)

Human Brain

Brain is the main coordinating centre of the body.

Parts of the Brain:

- **Forebrain**
- **Midbrain**
- **Hindbrain**

Forebrain

Controls:

- Voluntary actions
- Intelligence
- Memory
- Reasoning
- Emotions
- Receives sensory impulses
- Involved in thinking

Parts:

- **Cerebrum**: Largest part; center of thinking, memory, voluntary action
- **Thalamus**: Relay center for sensory signals
- **Hypothalamus**: Controls hunger, thirst, sleep, and emotions

Midbrain

- Controls involuntary actions such as:
    o Movement of head
    o Neck
    o Trunk

Hindbrain

- **Cerebellum**: Maintains posture and balance
- **Pons**: Involved in regulation of respiration
- **Medulla**: Controls involuntary actions like heartbeat and breathing

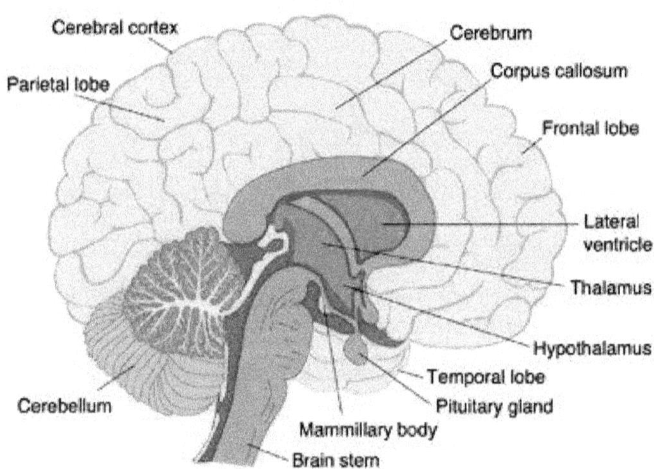

Protection of Nervous System

Brain

- Enclosed in **cranium** (bone box)
- Covered by **3 membrane layers** (meninges)
- **Cerebrospinal fluid** protects the brain from injuries

- Wrapped in **meninges**
- Protected by **vertebral column** (backbone)
- Vertebral column has **33 bones (vertebrae)**

More about Spinal Cord:

- Cylindrical extension of the brain, starts from **medulla**
- **31 pairs of nerves** arise
- Handles **spinal reflexes**
- Conducts **nerve impulses** to/from the brain

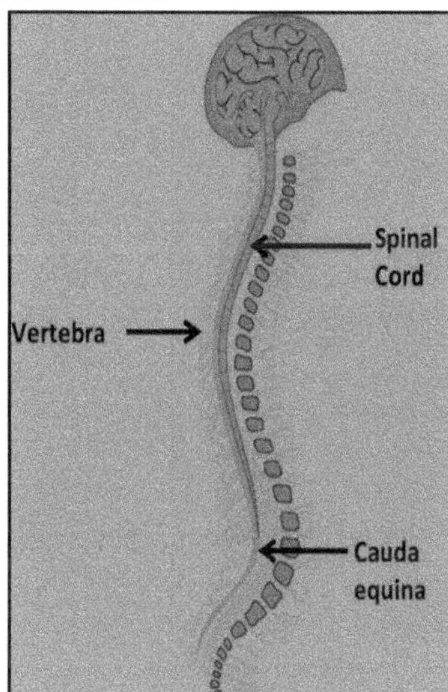

04.Chemical Coordination in Animals

Glands:

- Structures made of cells or tissues that secrete substances

Endocrine Glands (Ductless):

- Secrete substances directly into **bloodstream**
- Substances = **hormones**
- Hormones travel throughout the body
- Include: **Pituitary gland, thyroid, adrenal glands**
- Part of the **endocrine system**

Exocrine Glands:

- Secrete substances through **ducts**
- Substances act **near the target**
- Examples:
  - Sweat glands
  - Salivary glands
  - Gastric glands
  - Liver (bile)

Hormones:

- Chemical messengers in the bloodstream
- Regulate and control the activities of organs and tissues

Feedback Mechanism:

- Maintains **hormonal balance** by adjusting hormone secretion in response to changes in hormone levels

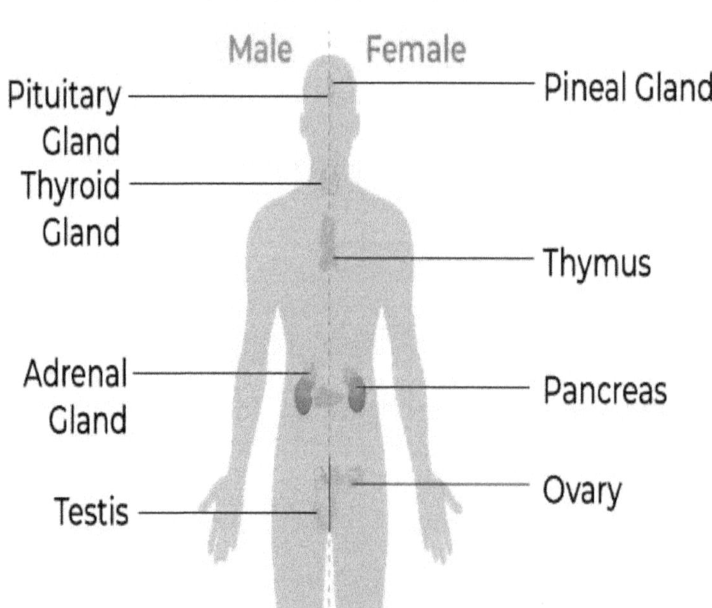

Gland	Location	Hormone	Function	Related Condition

Hypothalamus	Brain	Releasing & Inhibitory	Regulates pituitary gland hormones	-
Pituitary Gland	Below the brain	Growth Hormone	Controls body growth (bones, muscles) – *master gland*	Dwarfism, Gigantism
Thyroid Gland	Attached to windpipe	Thyroxine	Regulates metabolism of carbs, fats, and proteins	Goitre (iodine deficiency)
Parathyroid Gland	Embedded in thyroid gland	Parathormone	Regulates calcium and phosphate levels in blood	-
Thymus Gland	Lower neck / upper chest	Thymus Hormone	Develops immune system; large in children, shrinks after puberty	-
Pancreas	Below the stomach	Insulin & Glucagon	Regulates blood sugar levels; insulin helps glucose uptake	Diabetes

Adrenal Glands	On top of kidneys	Adrenaline	Prepares body for *fight or flight* (increases heart rate, energy use, etc.)	-
Testes	Male reproductive organs	Testosterone	Controls male puberty (voice, hair, etc.)	-
Ovaries	Female reproductive organs	Estrogen & Progesterone	Controls female puberty; progesterone supports pregnancy	-

04 Coordination in Plants

Type	Name	Description	Examples
Nastic (Not related to growth)	**Thigmonasty**	Non-directional movement in response to **touch**	*Mimosa pudica* (touch-me-not)
	Photonasty	Non-directional movement in response to **light**	*Dandelion, Moonflower*
Tropic (Related to growth)	**Phototropism**	Growth towards or away from **light**	—

	Hydrotropism	Growth in response to **water**	—
	Geotropism	Growth in response to **gravity**	—
	Chemotropism	Growth towards or away from **chemicals**	—
	Thigmotropism	Growth in response to **touch**	—

Nastic Movement vs Tropic Movement

Aspect	Nastic Movement	Tropic Movement
Direction	Non-directional response to stimuli	Directional response to stimuli
Speed	Fast movement	Slow movement
Plant Parts	Involves flat organs (e.g., leaves, petals)	Involves all plant parts

Plant Hormones (Phytohormones)

Plant Hormone	Functions
Auxin	Promotes cell enlargement, differentiation, and fruit growth. Controls response to light & gravity. Speeds up stem growth, slows root growth.
Gibberellins	Promotes cell enlargement & differentiation (with auxins), shoot elongation. Breaks seed and bud dormancy, promotes fruit growth.
Cytokinins	Promotes cell division, delays leaf aging, opens stomata, and promotes fruit growth. Breaks seed and bud dormancy.

Abscisic Acid (ABA)	Growth inhibitor, promotes seed and bud dormancy, closes stomata, causes leaf wilting, promotes detachment of flowers and fruits.

Question 1:
How does chemical coordination take place in animals?

Answer:

Chemical coordination takes place in animals with the help of hormones. Hormone is the chemical messenger that regulates the physiological processes in living organisms. It is secreted by glands. The regulation of physiological processes, and control and coordination by hormones comes under the endocrine system. The nervous system along with the endocrine system in our body controls and coordinates the physiological processes.

Question 2:
Why is the use of iodised salt advisable?

Answer:

Iodine stimulates the thyroid gland to produce thyroxin hormone. It regulates carbohydrate, fat, and protein metabolism in our body. Deficiency of this hormone results in the enlargement of the thyroid gland. This can lead to goitre, a disease characterized by swollen neck. Therefore, iodised salt is advised for normal functioning of the thyroid gland.

Question 3:
How does our body respond when adrenaline is secreted into the blood?

Answer:

Adrenalin is a hormone secreted by the adrenal glands in case of any danger or emergency or any kinds of stress. It is secreted directly into the blood and is transported to different parts of the body. When secreted in large amounts, it speeds up the heartbeat and hence supplies more oxygen to the muscles. The breathing rate also increases due to contractions of diaphragm and rib muscles. It also increases the blood pressure. All these responses enable the body to deal with any stress or emergency.

01 . Heredity

Definition: The process of passing down traits and characteristics from parents to their offspring through genes.

Variation

The difference between individuals in a species or group of organisms.

Types of Variation:
- Environmental variation
- Genetic variation

Importance of Variation

1. Variation helps organisms adapt to changing environments.
2. It drives the evolution of new, better-adapted species.

Accumulation of Variation During Reproduction

Asexually:
- Variation are fewer.
- Occurs due to small inaccuracies in DNA.

Sexually:
- Variation are large.
- Occurs due to crossing over, separation of chromosomes.

Genetics

The biological science that deals with the mechanism of heredity and causes variation is called genetics.

The term "genetics" was coined by English biologist William Bateson.

Father of Genetics: Gregor Johann Mendel

Acquired Traits vs Inherited Traits

Acquired Traits	Inherited Traits
a) Do not change germ cells	Bring changes in germ cells
b) Cannot be passed on to future generations	Can be passed on to their progeny
c) Do not lead to evolution	May lead to evolution
Example: Losing limbs due to an accident	Example: Deformed limbs at birth due to a genetic defect

Key Genetic Terms

- DNA (Deoxyribonucleic acid): A molecule that contains genetic information for the development and functioning of an organism.
- Chromatin: A mixture of DNA and proteins that form chromosomes in the cells of humans and other higher organisms.
- Chromosomes: A DNA molecule that consists of a part or all of the genetic material of an organism.
- Genes: A segment of DNA that is the basic unit of heredity and is passed from parent to child; contains genetic information for development and functioning.

Haploid vs Diploid Cells

Haploid Cells	Diploid Cells
Contain one set of chromosomes (n).	Contain two sets of chromosomes (2n).
Formed by the process of meiosis.	Undergo mitosis for division.
Examples: Sperm and egg cells.	Examples: Nerve and muscle cells.

Rules of Inheritance

- Inheritance in humans is influenced equally by paternal and maternal genes.
- Traits in children follow Mendel's rules of inheritance.
- Each child inherits one version of a trait from each parent.

Dominant Allele	Recessive Allele
The dominant allele is the stronger of the two alleles.	The recessive allele is the weaker of the two alleles.
Represented by a capital letter, it determines the dominant traits.	Represented by a lowercase letter, it remains suppressed in the presence of dominant.
Dominant traits manifest in both homozygous and heterozygous conditions.	Recessive traits are expressed only in the homozygous condition.

Homozygous vs Heterozygous

Homozygous Condition	Heterozygous Condition
Inherits identical alleles of a gene from both parents	Inherits different alleles of a gene from each parent

Genotype vs Phenotype

- Genotype: The unique DNA sequence or allele combination inherited from parents.
- Phenotype: Observable traits like appearance and behavior, influenced by genotype and environment.

02 .Gregor Mendel's Experiment

Plant selected by Mendel: Pisum sativum (garden pea)
Used a number of contrasting characters for garden pea.

Why only pea plant?
- Annual plant
- Short life cycle
- Choice of cross or self-fertilization
- Large number of offsprings
- 7 pairs of allelic characteristics

Mendel's Rules for the Inheritance of Traits

- Law of Dominance: In heterozygous pairs, the dominant allele masks the recessive one.
- Law of Segregation: Traits have two alleles that separate during gamete formation; one from each parent combines during fertilization.

- Law of Independent Assortment: Alleles of different genes assort independently into gametes.

03 .Mono Hybrid Cross

Cross between two pea plants with one pair of contrasting characters.

F1 Generation: All progeny were tall.
F2 Generation: Progeny of F1 included both tall and dwarf plants.
Tallness was expressed in F1, but both tallness and dwarfness were inherited.
Each organism inherits two copies of a trait, which may be identical or different based on parentage.

Monohybrid Cross Ratio:
- Phenotypic ratio: 3 Tall : 1 Dwarf
- Genotypic ratio: 1 TT : 2 Tt : 1 tt
Note: T (dominant), t (recessive).

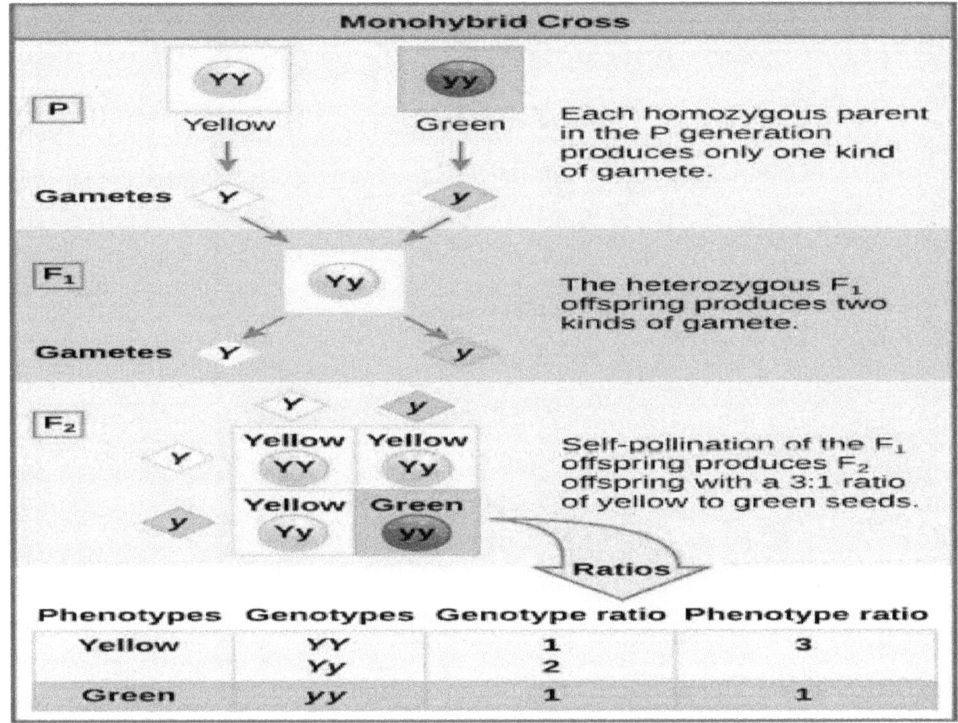

Phenotypes	Genotypes	Genotype ratio	Phenotype ratio
Yellow	YY	1	3
	Yy	2	
Green	yy	1	1

04. Dihybrid Cross

A cross between two plants having two pairs of contrasting characters.

Phenotype Ratio:
- Round, Yellow: 9
- Round, Green: 3
- Wrinkled, Yellow: 3
- Wrinkled, Green: 1
Parents: Round Green × Wrinkled Yellow

Self-pollination of F1 plants resulted in parental phenotypes and two new mixtures.

Round and Yellow seeds are dominant traits.

The appearance of new phenotype combinations indicates that the genes for round and yellow seeds are inherited independently.

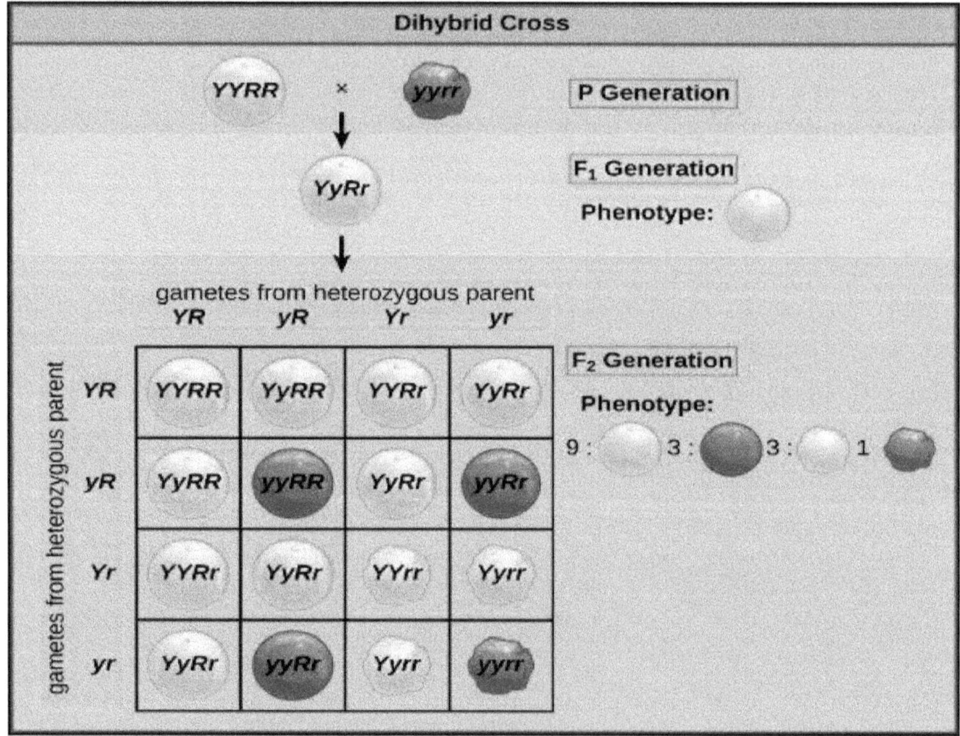

05.Sex Determination

The process through which the sex of a newborn individual is established.

Factors Affecting Sex Determination

1. Environmental:

- In certain animals, like turtles, the temperature at which fertilized eggs are kept determines the gender.

2. Genetic:

- In humans and other animals, gender is determined by a pair of sex chromosomes.

- Humans have 23 pairs of chromosomes:
  *** XX = Female**
  *** XY = Male**

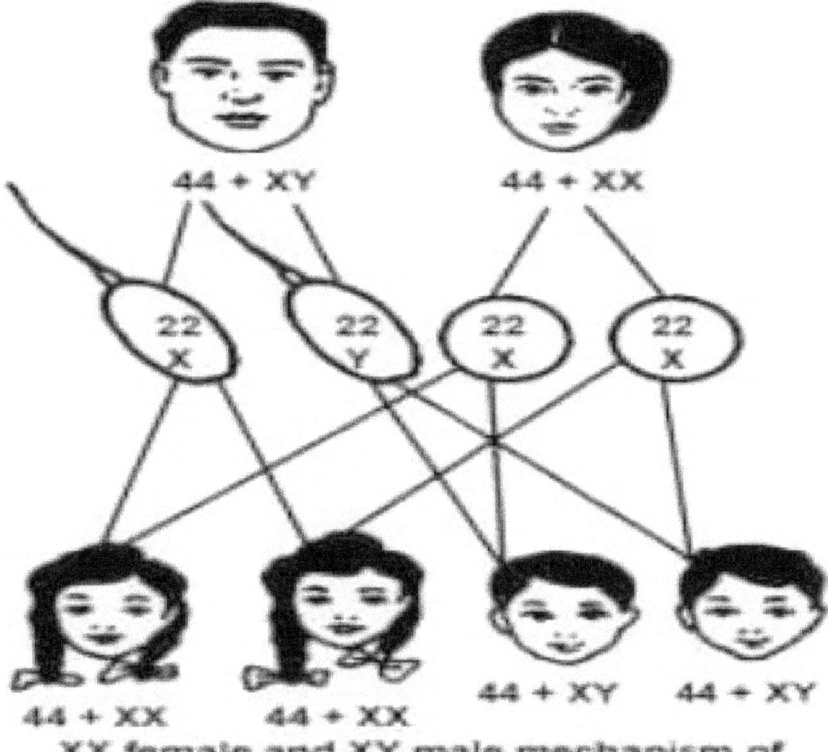

XX female and XY male mechanism of sex determination in human

Question no 01 ; What factors could lead to the rise of a new species?

Answer: Natural selection, genetic drift and acquisition of traits during the life time of an individual can give rise to new species.

Question 2: Will geographical isolation be a major factor in the speciation of a self-pollinating plant species? Why or why not?

Answer: Geographical isolation can prevent the transfer of pollens among different plants. However, since the plants are self-pollinating, which means that the pollens are transferred from the anther of one flower to the stigma of the same flower or of another flower of the same plant, geographical isolation cannot prevent speciation in this case.

Question 3: Will geographical isolation be a major factor in the speciation of an organism that reproduces asexually? Why or why not?

Answer: Geographical isolation prevents gene flow between populations of a species whereas asexual reproduction generally involves only one individual. In an asexually reproducing organism, variations can occur only when the copying of DNA is not accurate. Therefore, geographical isolation cannot prevent the formation of new species in an asexually reproducing organism.

Environment

01 .Environment:

- everything that is around us, which includes both living and nonliving things such as soil, water, animals and plants, which adapt themselves to their surroundings.

Ecosystem

- a community of living organisms and their physical environment that interact together in a specific area

Natural ecosystem

- The ecosystem which exist in nature on its own.
- Example: forest, lake, ocean.

Artificial ecosystem

- Man-made ecosystem.
- (Aquarium, Garden, Crop field etc.)

Aquatic

- Marinc
- Fresh water

Territorial

- Forest
- Desert

- Grassland

Components of Ecosystem

Biotic components (Living Organism)

- Autotrophs (Producers)
    - All green plants and blue green algae can produce their own food using abiotic factors.
- Heterotrophs (Consumers)
    - (i) Herbivores: Plant Eaters
    - (ii) Carnivores: Flesh Eaters
    - (iii) Omnivores: Eat both plants and animals e.g., human
- Decomposers
    - Include organisms which decompose the dead plants and animals. Example: fungi, earthworms

Abiotic components (Non living organisms)

- Physical factors
    - Air
    - Water
    - Minerals
    - Soil
- Chemical factors
    - Organic
        - Protein, fats
    - Inorganic
        - Hydrogen, Oxygen

Fundamental energy driving our climate system

- Sunlight

Environment

- The physical and biological surroundings where organisms live.
- Includes all the external conditions affecting an organism's life.
- Environment changes as an organism moves from one place to another.

- Focuses on the physical surroundings like air, water and land.
- Environment does not depend directly on life processes.

Ecosystem

- A system where living (biotic) and non-living (abiotic) components interact.
- Includes interactions like food chains, food webs, and nutrient cycles.
- Ecosystems remain stable regardless of an organism's movement.
- Focuses on interactions between biotic and abiotic factors like plants, animals, and sunlight.
- Ecosystems depend on processes like photosynthesis and decomposition.

How Ecosystem works?

Sunlight (Energy Source)

- Producers (Green Plants)
  - Use solar energy to convert carbon dioxide and water into organic matter through photosynthesis
  - Absorb minerals from soil.

Consumers

- Herbivores: Feed on plants (Primary Consumers)
- Carnivores: Feed on other animals (Secondary/Tertiary Consumers)

Decomposers

- Break down dead plants and animals
- Recycle carbon dioxide, water, and nutrients back into the soil, air and water

Nutrient Recycling

- Nutrients are reused by plants, completing the ecosystem cycle.

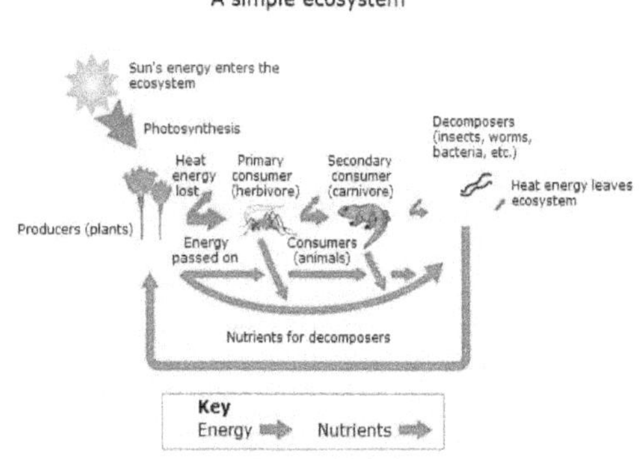

02. Food Chain:

- A series of organisms feeding on one another.(List of organisms which shows who eats whom)

Food Web:

- A food web is a network of interconnected food chains showing complex feeding relationships in an ecosystem.
- It demonstrates how each organism can be consumed by multiple organisms and vice versa.

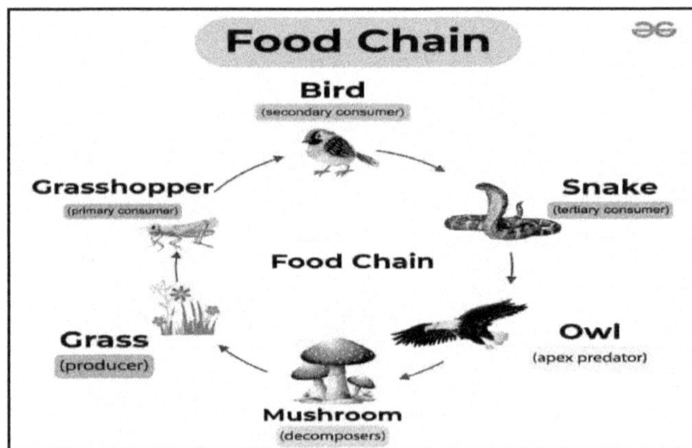

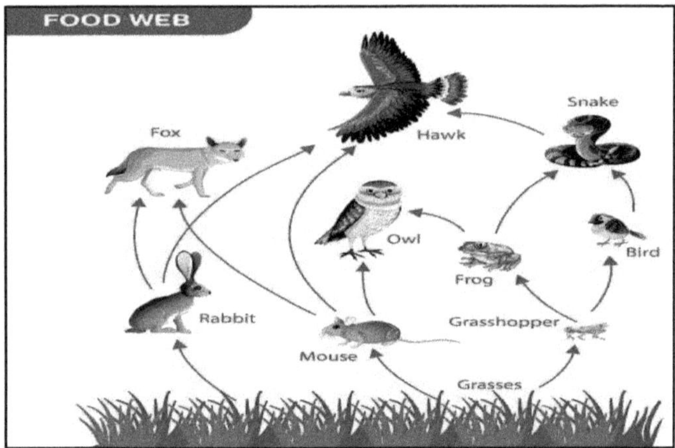

Trophic level

- It is the position an organism occupies in a food chain based on its role in the flow of energy
- First Level: Autotrophs/Producers (e.g., green plants)
  - Fix solar energy into chemical energy.
- Second Level: Herbivores/Primary Consumers
- Third Level: Small carnivores/Secondary Consumers
- Fourth Level: Larger carnivores/Tertiary Consumers

ENERGY FLOW:

- Energy flows through the environment via food chains.
- Producers capture sunlight and make it available to consumers and decomposers.
- Energy decreases at each trophic level, with only 10% of energy transferred to the next level.

The 10% law of energy transfer, proposed by Raymond Lindeman, states that only 10% of the energy from one trophic level is passed on to the next level in a food chain. The remaining 90% is lost as heat, during movement, growth, and other life processes.

KEY OBSERVATIONS ABOUT ENERGY FLOW:

- Green plants capture 1% of solar energy falling on their leaves.
- At each trophic level:
  - Heat loss: A large part of energy is lost as heat to the environment.
  - 10% Rule: Only 10% of the consumed energy is converted into biomass and made available to the next level.
- Due to energy loss, food chains are usually limited to 3-4 levels.
- Producers are the most numerous, with numbers decreasing progressively at higher trophic levels.

BIO MAGNIFICATION

- Progressive accumulation of harmful chemicals (e.g., pesticides) in organisms at higher trophic levels.
- Chemicals enter the food chain through soil or water (absorbed by plants/organisms).
- As these chemicals are non-degradable, they accumulate at each trophic level.

- Humans, being at the top of the food chain, accumulate the highest concentration of these chemicals.

Food Chain

- A linear sequence of organisms where each is eaten by the next organism.
- Simple and straightforward, showing one pathway of energy flow.
- Each organism is linked to only one other organism at the next trophic level.
- Less stable; affected if one organism is removed from the chain.
- Energy flows in a single direction (unidirectional).
- Example: Grass → Grasshopper → Frog → Snake → Hawk

Food Web

- A complex network of interconnected food chains in an ecosystem.
- Complex and branched, showing multiple pathways of energy flow.
- Each organism is connected to multiple organisms at different trophic levels.
- More stable; removal of one organism has less impact due to multiple connections.
- Energy flows through multiple interconnected pathways.
- Example: Grass is eaten by grasshoppers, rabbits, or deer, which are eaten by frogs, hawks, or lions.

04 .Ozone Layer and its Depletion:

The thickness of ozone layer is measured in DOBSON unit. The average total column is about 300 DU.

THE REGION WHERE TOTAL COLUMN OZONE DROPS BELOW 220DU=OZONE WHOLE (ANTARTIC)

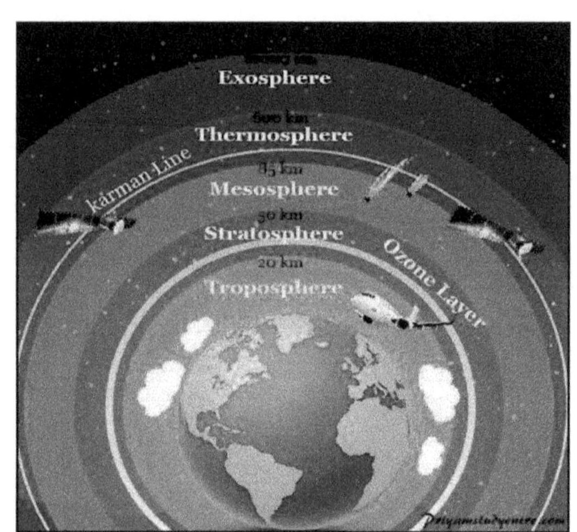

OZONE: Molecule made of three oxygen atoms.

- Protects Earth from harmful UV radiation, which can cause skin cancer in humans.
- Ozone is formed when UV rays split oxygen molecules (O_2), and free oxygen atoms combine with O_2 to form ozone (O_3):
    - $O_2 \rightarrow O + O$ (by UV rays)
    - $O + O_2 \rightarrow O_3$ (ozone formation)

Depletion of Ozone Layer:

- Sharp decline observed since the 1980s due to chemicals like Chlorofluorocarbons (CFCs) used in refrigerants and fire extinguishers.
- The UNEP (1987) introduced an agreement to limit CFC production at 1986 levels.

05.Garbage disposal:

Improvements in lifestyle have resulted in accumulation of large amounts of waste material.

Types of waste

- **Biodegradable**
    - Waste materials that can be broken down into simpler substances by natural processes such as the action of microorganisms (bacteria and fungi).
    - Examples: Food waste, paper, cotton, and vegetable peels.
- **Non biodegradable**
    - Waste materials that cannot be broken down by natural processes and remain in the environment for a long time.
    - Examples: Plastic, glass, and metals.

Harmful effects of waste

- Ozone depletion
- Air, soil and water pollution
- Bioaccumulation
- Bio magnification

Some methods of Waste disposal

- **Biogas plant:** Converts biodegradable waste into biogas and manure.
- **Sewage treatment plant:** Cleans drain water before releasing it into rivers.
- **Landfilling:** Buries and compacts waste in low-lying areas.
- **Composting:** Turns organic waste into manure in a compost pit.
- **Recycling:** Processes non-biodegradable waste into new items.
- **Reuse:** Uses items again, like making envelopes from old newspapers.
- **Incineration:** Burning waste at high temperatures to form ash, reducing its volume; commonly used for hospital waste.

CHALLENGES: Improper disposal of plastics and electronic waste harms the soil and water. Recycling processes, like for plastics, may also have environmental impacts.